Ministering Through Music

Ministering Through Music

Delton L. Alford

Edited by Donald S. Aultman

Church of God School of Ministry
Cleveland, Tennessee

Unless otherwise noted, Scripture quotations are from the King James Version of the Bible.

Scripture quotations marked *NKJV* are taken from the *New King James Version (NKJV)* of the Bible. Copyright © 1979, 1982, 1990, 1995, Thomas Nelson, Inc., Publishers.

Scripture quotations marked *NIV* are taken from the Holy Bible, *New International Version®*. *NIV®*. Copyright © 1973, 1978, 1984 by International Bible Society. Used by permission of Zondervan Publishing House. All rights reserved.

Paul L. Walker, Ph.D.
Chancellor, Division of Education

Donald S. Aultman, Ed.D.
Vice Chancellor, Division of Education
Director, School of Ministry

Homer G. Rhea, L.H.D.
Editorial Director

ISBN: 0-87148-623-7

Printed by Pathway Press
Cleveland, Tennessee

CONTENTS

FOREWORD

When, at age 18, I was invited to be the music director at the North Chattanooga Church of God in 1948, my primary qualifications were that I was a musician who could play the piano and wave my arms at the choir. At that time there were only two or three full-time music directors in the entire Church of God, so I was one of the first persons in the church to assume the role. This was long before there was a Department of Music Ministry in the church, and even though I had a strong interest in music, I had no model or mentor to help me understand the role of a music director or the potential of a music ministry. That situation would have continued in the denomination had it not been for people like Delton Alford, who, as a minister with a primary focus in music, dedicated his life to understanding the role of music in worship and promoting the ministry of a music director.

For more than a quarter of a century, the name Delton L. Alford has been synonymous with music in the Church of God. His influence on music in the church began when he came to Lee College (now Lee University) in 1962, from Florida State University, where he received the Ph.D. in music. As chairman of the Lee College Department of Music and conductor of the Lee Singers, Alford's impact on the denomination was wide and deep. His ability to conduct choral music was particularly impressive and revealed how adept he had become as a music teacher. After a career in college administration as dean of Arts and Sciences and vice president and dean of Lee College, Dr. Alford was called to direct the music fortunes of the entire denomination. He founded the church's first Department of Music Ministries where he continues his service to the Church of God.

During the entire span of his career, Alford has been involved in the creative side of music through writing, arranging, and producing. A prolific writer, he has authored several music collections and numerous octavos. Serving as founding president of SpiritSound Music, a church-related music firm, he produces Christian recordings for a wide range of artists. Outside of the denomination, Alford has impacted the Christian music community with service on numerous boards and committees and as an officer in the Church Music Publishers' Association. Among his many books and articles, he is a contributor to the *Dictionary of the Pentecostal/Charismatic Movement.*

The 14 chapters in this book are a distillation of Alford's intense feelings about the role of music in the ministry of the church, especially as music relates to worship. The original work was a series of video recordings which Alford presented as part of a video library curriculum for the School of Ministry's Certificate In Ministerial Studies (CIMS), designed for pastors and ministers. The material for this volume was transcribed from the video presentations and edited for publication in written form.

Many persons have contributed to the development of CIMS, particularly this course, *Ministering Through Music*. The church is indebted to Paul L. Walker who, as general overseer and chancellor of the Division of Education, saw the need for a School of Ministry. His value as a role model pastor for the Church of God during his 38 years at Mount Paran in Atlanta, included the skillful way he made use of music in worship. Appreciation is due Homer G. Rhea, editorial director of the School of Ministry, for his guidance on important matters from designing a cover to final publication. Abigail Hughes had the huge task of transcribing Alford's words from the original video recordings. Nellie Keasling was proficient in matters related to content and copyediting. Gwen Westfield flowed the text for the book. Barbara Fulbright, has been an invaluable aid in the production of the CIMS video library, where she serves as my associate producer for video production. LeAnn Morehead did the music typography and gave other valuable assistance to Dr. Alford. Not the least is my appreciation to Delton Alford for reading final drafts and making important additions to the edited text. Finally, a word of commendation goes to Mryna Alford, faithful wife and music collaborator with Delton. For many years, they have exhibited what it really means to be a team.

Donald S. Aultman
Vice Chancellor, Division of Education
Director, School of Ministry

June 2002

PREFACE

Upon learning that I would have the opportunity to teach a course in the School of Ministry CIMS series, I was delighted to immediately begin preparation for *Ministering Through Music.* My task was made even more rewarding when I discovered the video-teaching sessions were going to be edited for book publication. The ideas, reflections and recommendations presented in this book represent years of experience as a church musician, teacher, administrator, writer, music minister and worshiper. My first meaningful experiences in music were related to church worship and ministry. I made an early commitment to be involved in music and music ministry in response to the call of God on my life.

From those youthful performing experiences at the keyboard or in the church choir, band and various ensembles, I began to understand something of both the privileges and responsibilities of music ministry. Subsequent opportunities in higher education, as teacher, administrator and conductor afforded time for growth both as musician and minister. Practical issues relating to performance standards and techniques for volunteer church musicians were addressed through writing, arranging and conducting activities. A commitment to excellence in ministry and in music has been a lifelong pursuit made more intense by my growing awareness that the role music plays in Kingdom work is perhaps more important now than at any previous time

Although many different aspects of ministering through music are addressed in the text that follows, I have emphasized the importance of the role of true worship in the life of 21st-century believers. My own development as a worshiper has grown immensely in the last decade of my Christian experience. True worship is a high calling, and God is deserving of our highest praise. Hopefully, this book will encourage and enable both author and reader in increasingly effective music ministry to the "worship generation."

It is a pleasure to express thanks and appreciation to my colleague of many years Dr. Donald S. Aultman for his excellent editing of the manuscript and for valuable reactions and counsel. It has been a fruitful and rewarding musical journey since that occasion in 1967 when he invited me to author my first book on music ministry. LeAnn Moorhead, Administrative Assistant in the Department of Music Ministries, has given valuable assistance unselfishly. My wife, Myrna, has been witness and participant in a large number of the music experiences and ministry opportunities that have helped create the perspectives, understandings and principles upon which this narrative is based. I am grateful for her advice, vision, friendship and love.

This effort is meant to be more practical and personal than scholarly. It is given in thanks to God and appreciation for opportunities to be involved in ministry with students, choirs, orchestras, ensembles and congregations in developing skills and abilities that will produce powerful and anointed music in the worship, evangelism, education and nurturing ministries of the church.

Delton L. Alford, Ph.D.
Director, Music Ministries

May 2002

1

The Role of Worship

Perhaps the highest calling of the believer is that of worship. God seeks true worshipers, and Scripture makes it very clear that the praise and worship experience is a high priority. This book is presented as a study of music and its role in worship, both personal and corporate. Music has long been a vital part of the life of the believer, and in this time of intense emphasis on worship and its importance to the church and the individual, the examination of music and worship becomes even more relevant. Indeed, one of the most vital and significant areas of understanding for the church and today's minister is the role of music in the worship activities of the believer. Some have begun to refer to the generation of the first decade of the 21st century as the "worship generation," signifying its commitment to worship and its expressed hunger for God.

Following a brief study of the use and importance of music in the worship life of the Pentecostal/ Charismatic believer, current music types, forms and styles utilized in Pentecostal worship will be examined. With emphasis on discovering the role of music from a Scriptural perspective, the worship experience will be explored from Biblical and contemporary models of music in worship. Types and styles of music appropriate for worship will be noted, and attention will be given to the total role of music ministry in the church, not only as it impacts worship, but also as it impacts education, evangelism, and nurture.

The Biblical Model

The importance of music in the life of the believer is seen throughout Scripture. It is important to note that God, being a musician, ordained and created music to be a part of the total lifestyle of all believers.

1. *Music is an integral part of the universe.* It was born in the heart of God. Job 38:7, Isaiah 14:7 and 44:23 reveal that the heavens are filled with music and even the stars were made to sing. All creatures in the earth and in the heavens are made with musical skill and are commanded to praise the Almighty God. Indeed, the universe is a musical instrument created by God himself.

2. *God created music, both sacred and secular.* Exodus 15:1, 2, 20, 21 and Joshua 6:4, 5 indicate that in addition to worship, music had varied uses in the life of God's people. Music was used for sacred purposes, but it was also used in the secular

activities of the people—for work, recreation, celebration and even warfare. David danced before the Lord. Miriam sang a song of triumph. People worked in the fields to the sounds of music, and they also possibly sang as they navigated boats up and down the river. In addition, they engaged in war, accompanied by the sounds of their music.

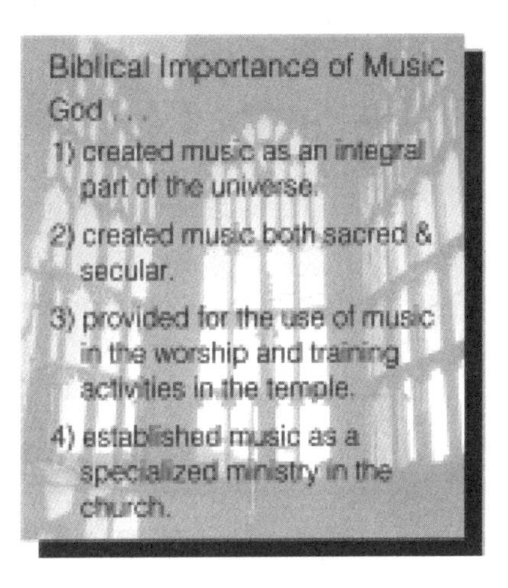

3. *God provided for the use of music in the Temple and the Tabernacle.* Second Chronicles 5:11-14, Psalm 100:1, 2, and Psalm 150 give indications of how music was used in the worship ministries of both.

When the Temple was dedicated, large numbers of both instrumental and vocal musicians gathered together. The scriptures indicate that when the musicians were of one mind and in one accord singing and playing together in unison—declaring that the Lord is good, His mercy is everlasting and endures forever—then the glory of the Lord came down into the Temple in the form of a cloud. God's presence was so intense that the priests could not even stand up to minister.

Music ministry included both vocal and instrumental performances and involved musicians and priests. It is important to observe that in God's plan, He set aside an entire tribe for ministry. The Levites were designated as that tribe, and He placed both the priests and the musicians in it. The Levites trained and produced music performers and worship leaders for the church. In public worship, the musical emphasis was on congregational participation.

4. *God established music as a specialized ministry.* First Chronicles 16:1-10, and 2 Chronicles 29:25-28 indicate that the Levites with exceptional musical skills were assigned responsibility for organizing, teaching, and performing music on a continuing basis. They became the administrators of the total music ministry. Chenaniah was known as the chief musician and music teacher. Asaph, Heman and Jeduthun, also highly skilled musicians, were involved in both the teaching and the performing process as they prepared others to join them in ministering to the Lord and leading the congregation in public worship services.

Music and the Contemporary Church

Music is perhaps used more extensively in the ministry of today's church than at any other time in history. Typically, from 30 to 50 percent of the Pentecostal/Charismatic worship service is devoted to music. Music also has its place in almost every other area of church activity. It would be a disappointment to attend a worship service or any other church activity without an opportunity to participate in the joy of music, born in the heart of God, being directed back to Him by His people.

The appeal of music to the emotions and lifestyles of this generation is undeniable. In his book, *The Magnetic Music Ministry*, Bill Owens states that the most significant influences to transcend cultural barriers worldwide are sports and music.[1] Music enjoys almost universal acceptance as a medium for corporate and personal expression in worship. The power of music is made even more effective in the worship service by the impact of both text and melody deftly welded together into one cohesive vehicle for praise and worship. Considering the power of music to influence culture it would be well for ministers and musicians alike, to develop musical models of excellence that ultimately will be effective in positively changing attitudes and behaviors. The Christian music community should be committed to producing and disseminating quality CDs, DVDs, cassettes, videos and other forms of musical expression that can be the catalyst for creating life-changing experiences.

In describing the importance of music to the church and its worship, Rick Warren, pastor of the Saddlebrook Community Church observes: "When you choose your music, you are determining exactly

[1]Bill Owens, *The Magnetic Music Ministry*, ed. Herb Miller (Nashville: Abingdon Press, 1996), p. 21.

whom you are going to reach. More than any other factor, tell me what the music in the church is, and I will tell you who that church will be able to reach and who it will not be able to reach."[2] That is an interesting proposition. The author is saying that if pastors will allow him to come to their services, or even without attending a worship service, if they will describe the kind of music presented in their churches, he will tell them the kind of people that attend their churches. It has been said that if a church sings nothing but hymns, the congregation is primarily made up of parishioners who are 50 years old or older. If churches want baby boomers in their congregation, they should use music appropriate to that generation and allow it to be participatory in style. If a church would like to have teenagers involved, then the music must have pop and jazz influences, along with other forms of contemporary music. If a church would have a multicultural congregation, there must be black gospel music, along with the sounds of urban, Latin, Caribbean and various other styles. To be sure, music is an important determinant of what the mix of the congregation is going to be. To have a blended congregation, it follows that there should also be a blended musical program. Why not choose to develop a body of believers in the church that will be much like the body that is going to be gathered around the throne of God in heaven?

---

[2]George C. Hunter III, *How To Reach Secular Young People* (Nashville: Abingdon Press, 1992), p. 151.

Bill Owens further comments that people gravitate to churches which relate to their life experiences and that quality music is often the reason for their return to worship a second time.[3] If the music is good, if it has quality, if it is professional in performance and anointed in its utterance, that might be a very good reason for people to return a second time to decide whether or not they would like to be a part of that worshiping community. Kennon Callahan states, "If only one thing in a church can go well, it is important that worship go extraordinarily well."[4] Music is a powerful force to influence thoughts, emotions, and behavior in worship. It is most important to understand the powers and advantages of music that allow leaders more effectively to bring people into the presence of an almighty God.

Defining Worship

Since worship and music are both ordained of God, it is vital to understand how the two are related. The act of worship is an essential ingredient of the Christian experience. It is required by God and desired by man in his quest for meaning in life. Worship may be highly personal or corporate in its nature. Both forms are provided for in the typical Pentecostal/Charismatic worship service. Something exists in the nature of man, his heart, his very

[3]Bill Owens, Ibid., p. 12.

[4]Kennon L. Callahan, *Twelve Keys to an Effective Church* (San Francisco: Harper, 1987), p. 48.

being that causes him to reach out to a higher power, to seek for a higher knowledge, to seek for a greater good—indeed, to seek for the presence of a living God so that he may worship in praise and adoration.

There are many concepts and definitions of worship or the recognition of the "worthship" of God. Dr. Robert E. Webber, in his book, *Worship Is a Verb*, indicates that worship is indeed just that. It is not something to be described. It is something to do. Worship is participatory. It is action that is generated by God and responded to by man.[5]

Bob Sorge, in *Exploring Worship*, presents several descriptions of worship—concepts that directly relate to the discussion which follows.

1. *Worship is conversation between God and man.* It is God contacting, God influencing, God speaking to men, and men responding directly to Him. It is interesting to note that a connection can be made between the use of music in worship and the use of other forms of communication in worship.

2. *Worship is giving to God the sacrifice He requires—our total selves.* He made the sacrifice for mankind, and in return, He expects individuals to give of their best . . . to give their highest praises. However, He does not just expect their highest praises, He expects their lives—their total selves to be given back to Him in worship.

3. *Worship is an affirmative response to the self-revelation of the triune God.* It is a way of saying, "I

[5]Robert E. Webber, *Worship Is a Verb* (Waco, Texas: Word Books, 1985), p. 12.

recognize God the Father, God the Son, and God the Holy Spirit, and I give affirmation to my belief in them. Further, my commitment to God is to follow after His Word and His precepts and to do His will in my life."

4. *Worship is one's heart expression of love, adoration and praise to God.* This powerful concept goes beyond just the intellectual and reaches inside to the real person, so that in a personal way, one may express love, adoration, and praise to God. God desires for His people to enter into this kind of relationship with Him.

5. *Worship is extravagant love and extreme obedience.* It is going beyond the usual. It is going beyond the normal and expressing one's love for God in word, thought, and deed. The love that one has for God and His Son, Jesus Christ, is shown in one's faithful actions in response to His Word and His presence.[6]

Worship is most concisely defined as communication—communication between God and man. Worship is two-part. It is bimodal. It is stimulus and response. Either as individuals or as members of a corporate body, people hear from God and then respond to Him. When they express themselves to Him in praise and adoration, or through a life lived sincerely for Him, He responds.

---

[6]Bob Sorge, *Exploring Worship* (Canandaiqua, New York: Bob Sorge, 1987), pp. 65, 66.

This communication with God may be expressed through acts of adoration, praise, prayer, repentance, self-humiliation, meditation, devotion, consecration and commitment. Indeed, all of these responses are desirable when individuals pour out themselves to the God who created, forgives, saves, keeps, directs, empowers, and gives them eternal life. In worship, they say to Him: "We love you; we praise you; we adore you; and we lift you up."

Common Distinctives of Worship and Music

In their book, *Music and Worship in the Church*, Lovelace and Rice argue that music and worship compliment each other so well because there are elements of both that are very similar and almost incapable of being separated.[7] Worship and music then share certain common distinctives.

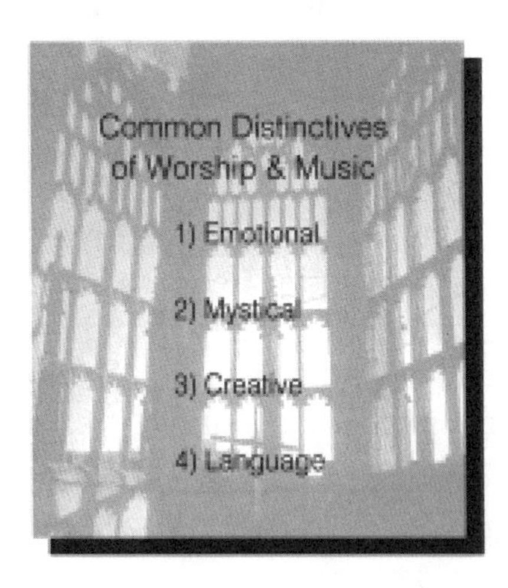

[7] Austin Lovelace and William C. Rice, *Music and Worship in the Church*, rev. ed. (Nashville: Abingdon, 1976), pp. 15-19.

1. *Worship and music are both emotional experiences.* Worship can best be understood when it is felt in the spirit—the soul of man—as is music. Music is often described by such phrases as, "It is beautiful . . . It is moving . . . It makes me want to laugh . . . It makes me want to cry." These emotional responses partner well with similar worship responses, and the two experiences share this commonality.

2. *Worship and music are both mystical.* It is difficult to define when worship occurs. There may be evidence of it in a smile, a tear, a raised hand or a hallelujah. There could be evidence of worship in a dance or when worshipers bow down, but all of these are merely evidences of the fact that something has happened. One cannot prove that worship occurred. One can feel only a need to demonstrate a proper response. Music response is much the same. One can say, "I love that music or I enjoyed that music," but that is a subjective evaluation that is somewhat mystical or "other worldly" in its derivation.

3. *Worship and music are creative.* Since both worship and music occur only within a specific time frame, they both provide opportunity for creativity when the experience reoccurs. This creative principle can be demonstrated in musical terms. When the same song is reprised, or the same chorus is repeated, or the same musical phrase occurs repetitively, there is opportunity for it to be changed or altered and thereby become a new expression or creative experience. Each time it can be new. In the same way, the worship experience is also creative. When worshipers come before the Lord and into His presence to worship, each experience ought to be

different, fresh, new—a creative experience involving the spirit and the mind.

4. *Worship and music have a language.* Worship has a language. It can be expressed by a body language indicating certain kinds of responses to God. It may be expressed in concepts or phrases such as, "Raise your hands . . . Clap your hands . . . Bow before the Lord . . . Come humbly into His presence." Worship also has a language of form and feeling. Music is often characterized as the universal language. Music has a language of melody, form, and feeling that is universally expressed regardless of culture or linguistics. The language of music transcends all communication and cultural barriers. Thus, music becomes a powerful medium for the expression of worship.

The Importance Of Worship

Christ himself speaks of the importance of worship in John 4:23 when He says, "But the hour is coming, and now is, when the true worshipers will worship the Father in spirit and truth; for the Father is seeking such to worship Him" (*NKJV*). This passage suggests three aspects of true worship.

1. *True worship is inspirational.* The spirit of man communicates with the Spirit of God. Something within him reaches out to the Spirit of God, particularly when he is breathed upon by the Holy Spirit. Inspiration touches language, and words convey new meaning. The Holy Spirit inspires individuals to speak and write the precepts, values, doctrines, beliefs, and lives of the people of God who, directed by the Word of God, and inspired by the

Spirit of God, are inspired to worship in spirit and in truth.

2. *True worship is intentional.* It is amazing, awe-inspiring, and humbling to think that the God of the universe seeks to communicate with His people. It is affirming to the individual believer to understand that an awesome God intends to bring His people into a worshiping relationship with Him. It then becomes the responsibility of the individual to seek time for worship of God. With intention, believers take time from their schedules for both personal and corporate worship. They intentionally move toward Him so that they can worship Him in spirit and in truth.

3. *True worship is invitational.* In worship, Christ is lifted up so that He can draw all people to Him. In His presence, men and women are drawn to Him for forgiveness of sins, for the building of relationships, and for the promise of an eternity of fellowship with the heavenly Father.

Music brings meaning and significance to the worship experience. It is a means of uniting the congregation in fellowship and in communion. It gives expression to the beliefs and the commitments of the church body. It draws the believers' hearts and thoughts to God. Music serves as a powerful vehicle for bringing the individual or the corporate body—through the anointing and the direction of the Holy Spirit—directly into the very presence of God. When music is offered as sincere praise to God and when it is enabled by the Holy Spirit, it becomes a significant part of true worship.

2

The Worship Experience

The 21st century began with a renewed interest and participation in worship, but it also witnessed much diversity and even controversy concerning the proper form or design of the public worship service. The enthusiastic disciples of praise and worship challenged proponents of traditional worship. Several subgroups of both persuasions engaged in vigorous debate over the most appropriate worship and music styles. The following examines what might be termed the complete worship experience from the perspective of a Biblical passage that elucidates both the essence and design of worship. Isaiah 6:1-9 presents a beautiful picture of worship in this context.

> In the year that King Uzziah died, I saw the Lord sitting on a throne, high and lifted up, and the train of His robe filled the temple. Above it stood the seraphim; each one had six wings: with two he covered his face, with two he covered his feet, and with two he flew. And one cried to another and said: "Holy, holy, holy is the Lord of hosts; the whole earth is full of His glory!" And the posts of the door were shaken by the voice of him who cried out, and the house was filled with smoke. So I said: "Woe is me, for I am undone! Because I am a man of unclean lips, and I dwell in the midst of a people of unclean lips; for my eyes have seen the King, the Lord of hosts." Then one of the seraphim flew to me, having in his hand a live coal which he had taken with the tongs from the altar. And he touched my mouth with it, and said: "Behold this has touched your lips; your iniquity is taken away, and your sin purged." Also I heard the voice of the Lord, saying: "Whom shall I send, and who will go for Us?" Then I said, "Here am I! Send me." And he said, "Go, and tell [the] people" (*NKJV*).

The Complete Worship Experience

Apart from the graphic picture of the majestic presence of the Lord, this passage contains three important principles, each with two parts, related to the complete worship experience. Worship is not just celebration and not just praise and worship. It is a continuum of various acts by the people of God responding to the presence of God. Isaiah states that he saw the Lord only after Uzziah died, and he finally focused on the Almighty God rather than the earthly king who had been his source of support. The acts of worship shown in this passage form the basis for understanding the total worship experience.

1. *Complete worship includes praise and adoration.* Isaiah saw the Lord, high and lifted up, with angelic beings singing, "Holy, holy, holy is the Lord of hosts." In the presence of this majesty and glory, Isaiah, too, was drawn to praise and celebrate the holiness of God. Here is the first two-part act of worship—the act of *praising God* and *adoring Him.* Anyone can offer praise, even a sinner, but the believer can go further by expressing personal adoration to the Lord. Music is a natural way to accomplish this aspect of worship. Songs that express praise and adoration include: "We Bow Before You," "Praise to the Lord," "All Hail the Power of Jesus' Name," "Glory to His Name," "What a Mighty God We Serve," "I Love You, Lord," "Lord, I Worship You," "Holy Is the Lamb," and many others.

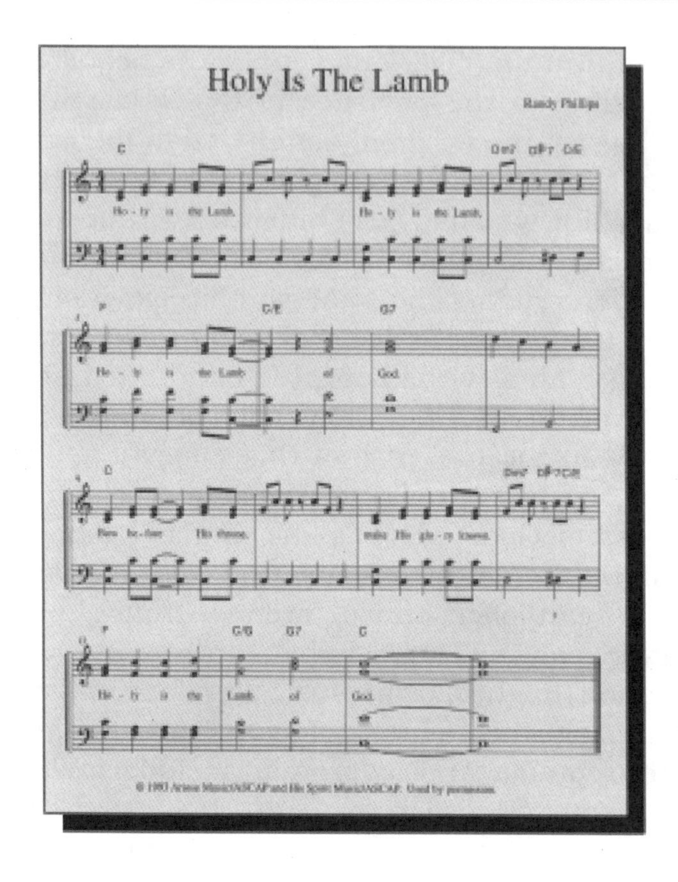

Upon examination, it can be seen that "Holy Is the Lamb" is an expression of praise. This praise chorus repeats the phrase, "Holy is the Lamb of God" throughout, calling also for the listener to bow before the throne and make His glory known. It is usually performed in an upbeat, energetic manner, with the rhythm accenting the text.

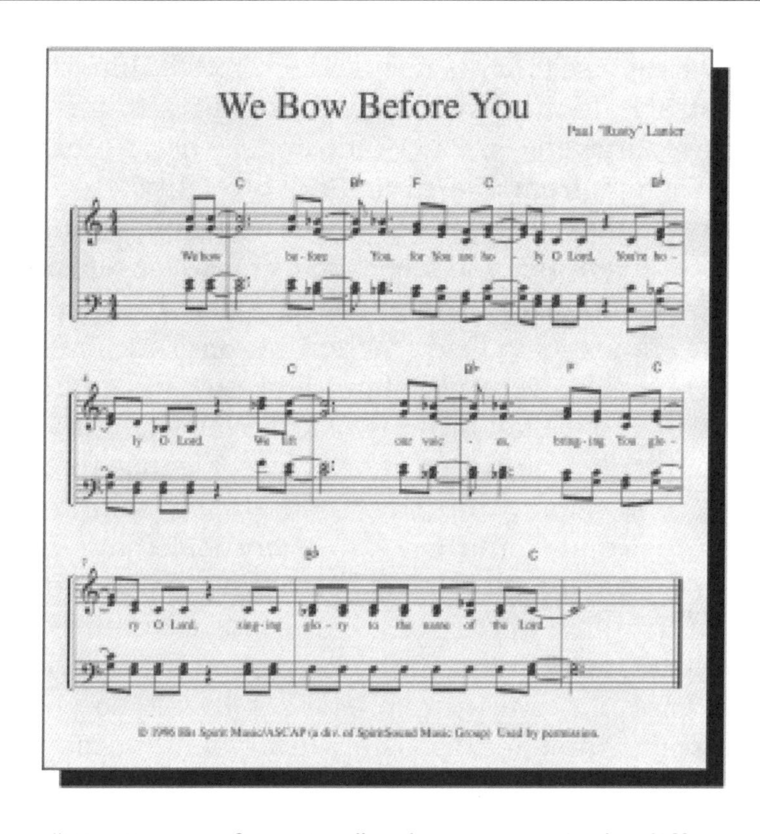

"We Bow Before You" takes an entirely different approach to worship through praise and adoration. The text indicates an attitude of submission and reverence. The music is usually performed in a reflective manner, but it may also be majestic in character. Whether believers are excited, involved, and moving at a rapid pace, or whether they are reflective, contemplative and moving at a moderate pace makes no critical difference; it is the worship aspect of praise and adoration that is important

2. *Complete worship includes the acts of humility and purification.* When the prophet saw himself in comparison to the holiness of God, he realized his

unworthiness and his need to bow before Him, to fall prostrate, to humble himself and to ask for and receive forgiveness. Then, the angelic being took the coal of fire from the altar and brought it to him. There ought to be opportunity in worship not only to praise, celebrate, and feel good but also for reflection and repentance. There should also be time for believers to say to God: "When we see Your majesty and holiness, we understand just how insignificant we are, and we fall humbly before You. Examine our thoughts and attitudes. Forgive us, cleanse us, and restore us again to a right relationship with You." Perhaps, one would say, "I do not feel that I need forgiveness today. I have not consciously sinned." Even if that were true, corporate worship calls believers to pray not only for personal forgiveness but also for everyone present. In all corporate worship, someone, possibly everyone, needs forgiveness for the sin of failing. A significant aspect of Pentecostal worship has been, and ought to continue to be, a time reserved for believers to reconcile themselves before the Lord in humility and ask for forgiveness and cleansing. Songs appropriate during this time of worship include: "Cleanse Me," "Open the Eyes of My Heart, Lord," "I Surrender All," "Spirit of the Living God," "Pour Out Your Anointing," "I Worship You, Almighty God," "Just As I Am," and "Holy Spirit, Fill Us."

Two examples of this type of song follow.

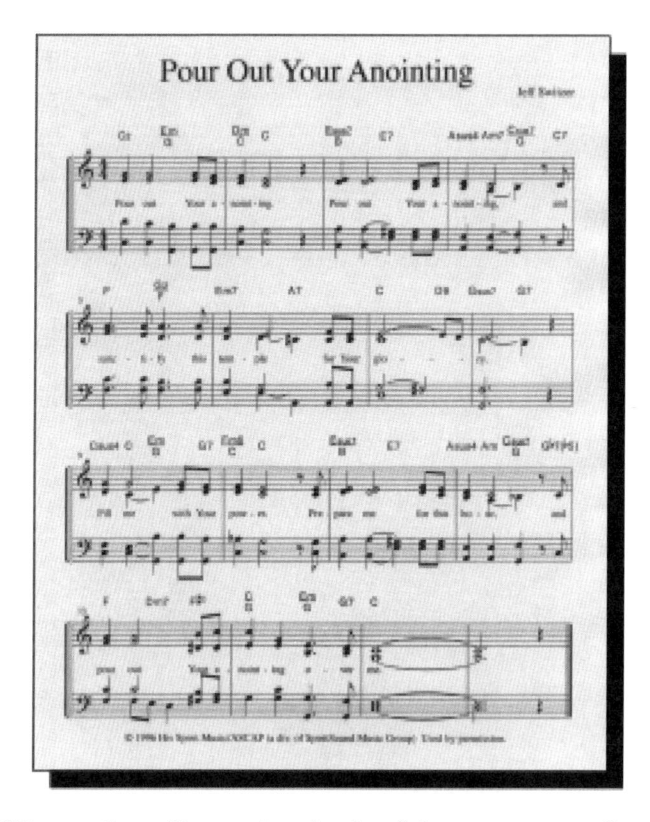

"Pour Out Your Anointing" is a prayer for the Holy Spirit to cleanse and anoint the human temple again. In the ancient Temple service, before public worship, the priest would present himself before the laver of cleansing for purification. Likewise, he would cleanse the vessels, applying oil to them, so they would be renewed for worship. When believers worship God, one of the acts of worship is to ask for forgiveness and cleansing.

"Holy Spirit, Fill Us" is a prayer for blessing and an outpouring of the power of the Holy Spirit. The text is positive and even somewhat forceful. The rhythms are syncopated, and the harmonic progressions are contemporary; therefore, the music is usually performed in an urban or black gospel style. Performing in this style allows both singers and instrumentalists to joyfully seek the cleansing and power of the Holy Spirit: "Holy Spirit, come, shower down blessings and fill us once again."

3. *Complete worship is an act of consecration and commitment.* Anointed with a coal of fire upon

his lips, Isaiah committed himself with these words: "Here am I! Send me." Being consecrated for service and committing oneself to service in the world are necessary components of worship. Believers must exalt Him and magnify His holy name, but that is not enough. They must be in a righteous relationship with the Lord—forgiven and purified—but even that is not enough. After praise and adoration, after forgiveness and cleansing comes consecration and service. As the worship experience moves to completion, worshipers have opportunity to communicate with God in perhaps the most powerful manner possible—they go out into the world to serve Him and do His work.

Songs useful in this time of worship include: "Yes, Lord, Yes," "Order My Steps," "Tell Them," "The Enemy's Camp," "I Am Thine, O Lord," "The Potter's Hand," "Where He Leads Me," "Make Me a Blessing," and "I'll Go Where You Want Me to Go."

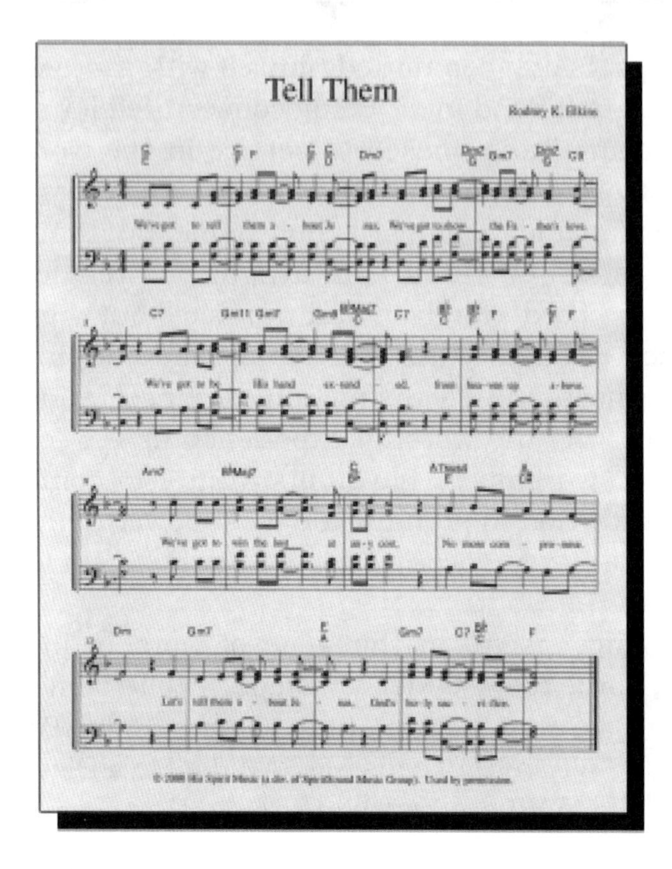

“Tell Them” is a wonderful expression of the need for personal commitment to evangelism. The world needs to hear about Jesus Christ. The joy, the responsibility, and the calling of the Christian are to tell the lost about Jesus Christ. In this example, both text and tune are contemporary in nature, but the message is timeless.

In the beautiful song, "The Potter's Hand," the believer says, "Lord, I place myself, I place my life into your hands. Mold me, change me, empower me, and cleanse me. Whatever you want to do with me, Lord, I set myself aside to be used at your direction." There is need for this kind of consecration in the complete worship experience.

These three, two-part acts of worship may not always occur in the same order. The sequence may change, but each is a necessary aspect of the complete worship experience. In order to worship

Him in spirit and in truth, there should be a time to praise and adore Him, to humble oneself before Him for forgiveness and purification, and to consecrate one's human vessel for commitment to Him for His service.

Musical Types in Worship

After defining the role of music in worship and considering the design of a complete worship experience and how music is an appropriate vehicle for helping accomplish such, the types of music appropriate to the worship experience itself will be discussed in this chapter. Scripture provides clear direction concerning the types of music which must be used in the various ministries of the church, including the ministry of worship. Variety in musical types and forms is a strong characteristic of Pentecostal worship music that derives from the New Testament. Throughout the history of the Pentecostal Movement, there has been extensive use of a variety of musical types the hymn, gospel hymn, gospel song, chorus, scripture song, and praise chorus are all part of the large repertoire enjoyed by both congregations and individuals.

The requirement for acceptance of the diversity of musical types is found in Paul's writing in two different passages: Colossians 3 and Ephesians 5. In both passages, Paul suggests at least three different types of songs or texts that should be used in church. In Colossians 3:16, he writes: "Let the word of Christ dwell in you richly in all wisdom, teaching and admonishing one another in psalms, hymns and spiritual songs, singing with grace in your hearts to the Lord" (*NKJV*). In Ephesians 5:18,19, Paul observes: "Be filled with the Spirit, speaking to one another in psalms and hymns and spiritual songs, singing and making melody in your heart to the Lord" (*NKJV*). Music historians have corroborated the fact that the early Christian practice of using a variety of song types did indeed occur. It was commonplace, including the practice of spontaneously singing spiritual songs, which were sometimes sung "in the Spirit" or "in tongues." From Scripture, one can conclude that the worship experience will be comprised of a variety of song types or forms, which will certainly include psalms, hymns and spiritual or gospel songs. A detailed look at these song types or forms and texts illustrates that each reveals the power and diversity of this Biblically based principle of variety. The following discussion will examine each of these types.

The Psalm

The *psalm* simply means "to sing the Word of God or to sing a paraphrase of Scripture." In the singing of a psalm, God speaks to believers directly.

Music has the ability to both send forth the Word and at the same time make it easy for the singer or listener to remember that Word. A melody linked to text can make it easier to memorize that text. Therefore, when singing His Word, one hears directly from Him, and hides that Word in his heart. Musical examples of this type are “Rejoice and Be Glad,” based on Psalm 118:24 and “I Will Call Upon the Lord,” based on Psalm 40.

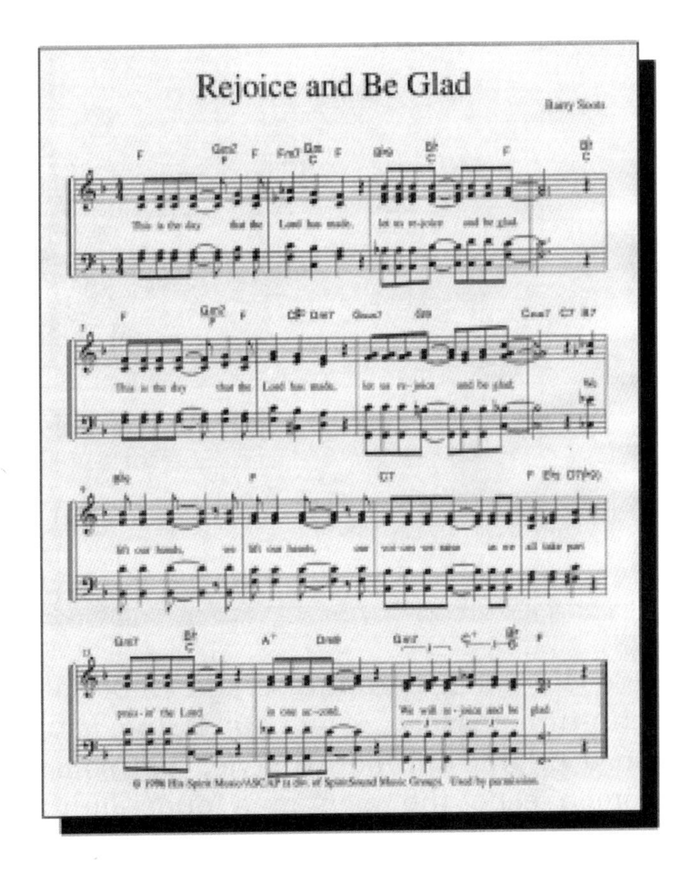

This psalm is a contemporary setting based on Psalm 118:24. It is also a paraphrase of Scripture. The song is usually performed in a very energetic manner and is often repeated several times for emphasis.

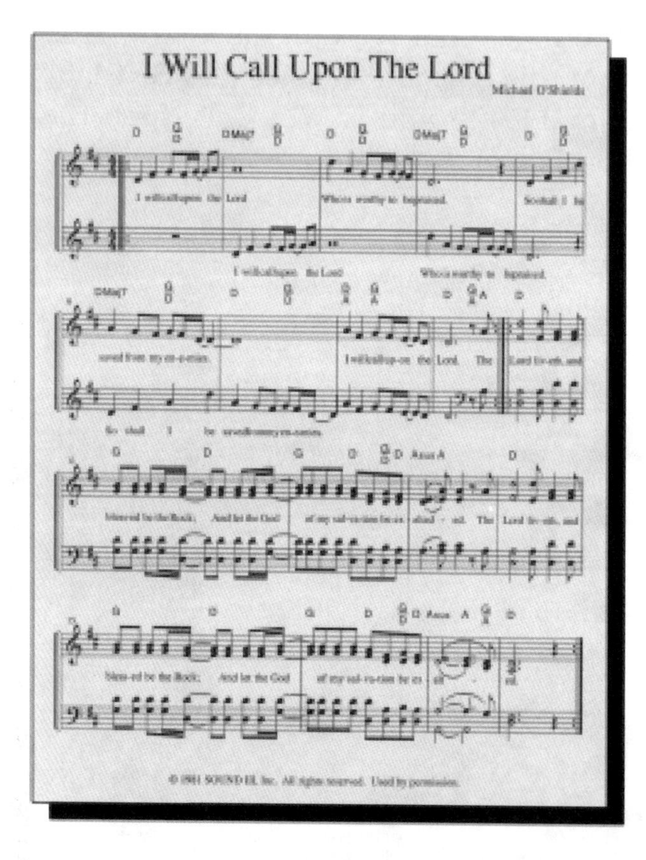

Here is another paraphrase and embellishment of a Scriptural passage, Psalm 40. It, too, is usually sung in a bright, affirmative style, and sometimes the women echo the men in a quasi-antiphonal manner, ever so slightly recalling the responsive and antiphonal singing in the Temple. Use of these two examples should not be taken to imply that all Scripture choruses ought to be performed in an upbeat manner or in a fast tempo. The issue of tempo and style, together with principles relating to variety in style and in tempo, will be discussed later.

The psalm, praise chorus and Scripture song are often composed through form, or they may be written in a simple two-part form, to be easily repeated. This two-part form often consists of the statement and answer phrases so typical of Old Testament psalm narrative. The contemporary psalm or chorus may also have a bridge or a contrasting thought added between repetitions of the main text. This allows for variety and creativity.

The Hymn

The *hymn* is a song of praise sung unto God, or it may be a song about the attributes of God. Believers hear from God by singing His Word. They also have opportunity as believers to respond to God in the singing of a hymn. Worshipers sing songs of praise and adoration directly to Him or sing songs that talk about Him, His attributes, or the beliefs and doctrines of the church.

Here are two songs that illustrate differing versions of the hymn.

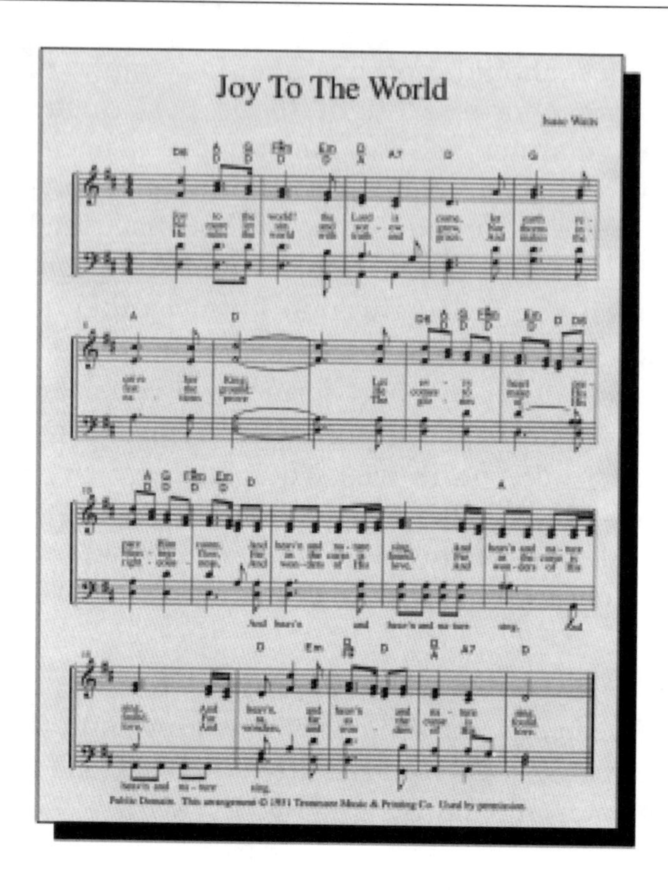

The first example, "Joy to the World," a traditional Christmas hymn, is a joyous telling of the good news of the birth and power of Jesus Christ. This hymn is written in strophic form, i.e., multiple verses set to the same melody. Strophic or verse form is typical of the hymn. The text extols the attributes and power of the Lord.

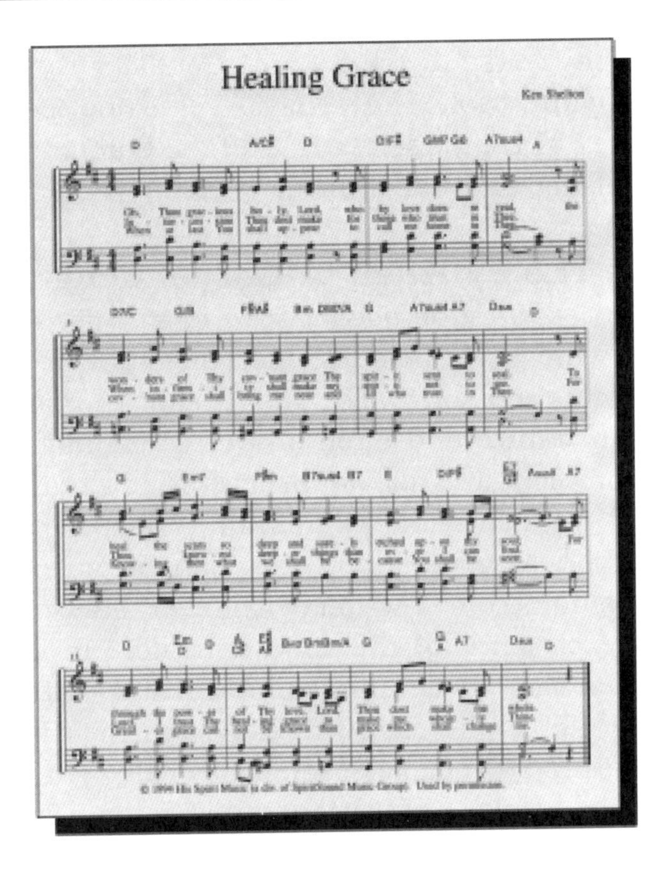

The second example is a contemporary version of the hymn. "Healing Grace" is also strophic in form with each successive verse describing the grace and the power of God. In performance the energy and tempo of the two songs are quite different. "Joy to the World" is a traditional hymn, joyously proclaiming Jesus, while "Healing Grace" is a contemporary hymn quietly expressing the grace and the power of God.

Like these two examples, the hymn is usually strophic in form, using a repeated melody for each successive verse of the hymn. Consider the traditional hymn, "Holy, Holy, Holy." Verse one speaks of God the Father, verse two of God the Son, and verse three of God the Holy Spirit.

The Spiritual or Gospel Song

The *spiritual* or *gospel song* is a song of testimony, which may be sung spontaneously or it may be a composed song. The gospel song is more personal in nature and often shares a testimony that has commonality for all believers. It may have started as a folk-like expression, passed on from generation to generation, or it can be an original composition from a writer wishing to share a personal experience of the Christian life. In singing these songs, believers communicate with one another about the blessings of God in their lives.

These types of gospel songs have always enjoyed a prominent place in Pentecostal worship. The gospel song brings a freshness and vitality to worship. It witnesses to the reality that Jesus is who He says He is and that He does what He says He will do. These three types of songs seem to be what Paul envisioned in worship. Early Church historians corroborate the fact that all three types were used in New Testament worship.

There are numerous examples of gospel songs, providing powerful testimony of the power and grace of God.

"He's Been So Good" testifies about the Holy Spirit, His blessings and power. The beauty of this song is that it provides a testimony common to believers, which can be shared corporately.

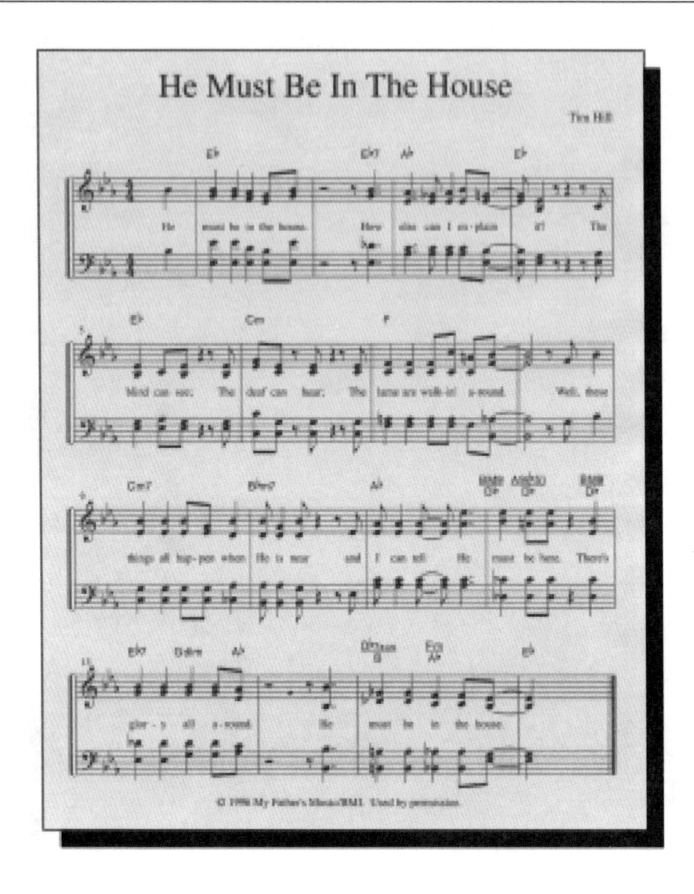

"He Must Be in the House" is a more traditional gospel song. It also excitedly proclaims the power of God and predicts that miracles will occur when Jesus comes into the place and touches people. This is a testimony that when Jesus arrives, special things happen. There is joy, excitement, blessing, and renewal. There is healing taking place, so, He must be in the house.

The gospel song usually takes the form of verse and chorus. The chorus is often designed to be repeated. Historically, many of these choruses have become stand-alone entities, and the performer or worshiper does not sing the verses, only the chorus. Typically, the storyline or theme of the song is presented in the verse, and the response of the chorus is to provide an embellishment of the theme. The gospel hymn is a musical song form that exhibits aspects of both the hymn and the gospel song. Examples of this type include: "Glory to His Name," "How Great Thou Art," and "Amazing Grace."

It is easy to understand the appeal of this music. The worshiper can often feel the joy and the anointing of the singers as they testify about the spiritual life. Not just the singers, however, the instrumentalists also have the opportunity to perform skillfully and prophetically before the Lord and to musically interpret and translate the joys of the Christian experience in their playing.

Contemporary versions of the chorus, gospel song and gospel hymn have brought some changes in form as well. Each of these types sometimes makes use of a bridge or contrasting musical or textual idea, thereby providing for variation and creativity.

Based on the Colossians and Ephesians passages, one can conclude that there are prescribed types of music for worship. When they are performed, there are no absolutes regarding tempo, that is to say, the speed of the presentation. Neither are there prohibitions as to style. Styles of music in worship may be as varied as traditional, contemporary, classical, Southern gospel, Black gospel, Caribbean, Latin, pop, folk, country, urban, or a combination of any of these and various others. The Scripture says absolutely nothing about musical styles and their appropriateness for worship or their place in a Christian lifestyle. Musical choices are individual, corporate or cultural, and they may vary from service-to-service, function-to-function, or even according to the age or the demographic make-up of the worshipers. Paul's recommendation for worship is to include psalms, hymns, and spiritual songs in the ministries of the church. Any musical style done sincerely in worship to God can be used to perform any of these.

4

A Word-Centered Music Ministry

The Scripture prescribes types of music to be used in worship, but remains silent concerning musical style—thus making allowance for age preferences, generational differences, and cultural diversity. Tolerance is extended for variety in musical preference, making possible the apt use, in various worship contexts, of music—both sacred and secular—from the popular culture of today. While being permitted diversity of musical style, believers are drawn together by the Word of God and a music ministry centered in the Word.

The Biblical Perspective

Two passages of Scripture, Colossians 3:16 and Ephesians 5:18-20, indicate the usefulness of music in the four primary ministries of the church. In these passages, one finds an outline for music ministry that is relevant for the contemporary church. The primary ministries identified for today's church are worship, evangelism, education, and nurture.

Ministry of worship

The references to "singing with grace" and "making melody in your heart to the Lord" in Colossians and Ephesians are calls to worship. Both admonitions can be described and understood as the action of an individual singing to the Lord in worship. This gives an understanding of how music supports the worship ministry of the church. The ministry of worship exalts God and praises Him for His awesome power and His glory. In exalting Him, the ministry of worship develops both the individual and the community of faith.

Ministry of education

Colossians instructs: "Let the word of Christ dwell in you richly in all wisdom, teaching and admonishing one another" (3:16). This reference to education and the teaching ministries of the church places the Word at the center of everything that is done. Through training and teaching, people grow "richly" in the faith. The worship ministry primarily edifies God, but the educational ministries of the church edify others by teaching them about God and the doctrines and beliefs of the Christian faith. Music is a powerful tool to be used in the educational ministries designed for children, youth, and adults of the church. Discovering the aspects of the triune

God, learning the truths of salvation, and understanding the triumphant Christian life are all facilitated by the effective use of music. A song, written by the well-known gospel composer Bennie S. Triplett, illustrates the potential use and lasting effect of Word-centered music education. It is based on the familiar verses from Proverbs 3:5, 6: "Trust in the Lord with all thine heart; and lean not unto thine own understanding. In all thy ways acknowledge him, and he shall direct thy paths." Coming to know this text and associating the beautiful melody, can provide a learning experience, which may well result in a permanent memory of the passage from Proverbs.

Ministry of evangelism

Paul's desire was that "the word of Christ dwell in [us] richly," not only in teaching but also in admonishing one another through music—psalms, hymns, and spiritual songs. One of the meanings of the word admonish is "to warn or gently reprove." The implication is that music can enable the message of the Word as it gently reproves both sinners and believers. When music is used in the evangelism ministry of the church, its form, emotion and meaning combine with the aural, intellectual and emotional responses of the listener in helping bring people to God, convicting them of sin, and convincing them of the necessity of the godly life.

> I'll never forget an experience I had as a struggling young Christian. In my teen years, already in college, I was having

difficulty with the church, my family, my relationship to God, and I was just generally frustrated. At home, on a weekend visit from college, I was sitting up all night watching TV and doing what we now call channel surfing. Accidentally, I switched channels from a ball game to a gospel singer. The cameras zoomed in on the face of an elderly gentleman as he sang these words: "Just a closer walk with Thee. Grant it, Jesus, is my plea. Daily walking close to Thee, let it be, dear Lord, let it be." I was moved by the words of that song. There in the quiet of the den of my dad's home, I suddenly realized that the problem wasn't the church or my family. The problem was not with God or His Word; I was the problem. I had drifted away from a close walk with the Lord. I needed to be convicted of my terrible attitude, and I needed to follow closely after Christ rather than from afar. At that moment, I went to my knees for forgiveness, and the Lord gave me the assurance that I had been restored. The next morning was a new day for me. At the breakfast table, my dad asked, "How are you feeling, son?" When I responded, "I'm feeling great, Dad," he was surprised and delighted. That was the first positive response he had heard from me since I had returned home from college. The chorus of one simple song, delivered sincerely, had moved me to change my life.

Music has power to convict, to reprove, and to reach an unbelieving world for Jesus Christ.

Ministry of nurture

Paul exhorts believers to speak to one another through music: "Speaking to one another in psalms and hymns and spiritual songs" (Ephesians 5:19, *NKJV*). Here the writer is promoting the use of music for communicating and sharing with one another. This can be seen as part of the caring or nurturing ministry of the church. In this case, believers are building up one another by the communication of the joys of the Christian life and by demonstrating the love of Christ as they attempt to meet one another's needs. Much of the music of the church communicates care for one another and belief in one another.

An increasingly important area of ministry concern is the individual's use of music in private and in the home. The impact of both sacred and secular music on today's believer is nothing less than awesome. Perhaps never before has music permeated the entire society like it does today. In 2001, income revenue from the sale of recorded CDs and cassettes in the United States exceeded the gross national product of more than 60 countries.

Music is everywhere. It is in the home, the mall, the restaurant, and the arenas of the world. Almost every venue one enters is constantly filled with the sounds of music. Music ministers have a huge opportunity for influence and guidance of Christians in their music leisure activities. In reviewing the following illustration, one can readily see the design of a Word-centered music ministry and its relationship with various other ministries of the local church.

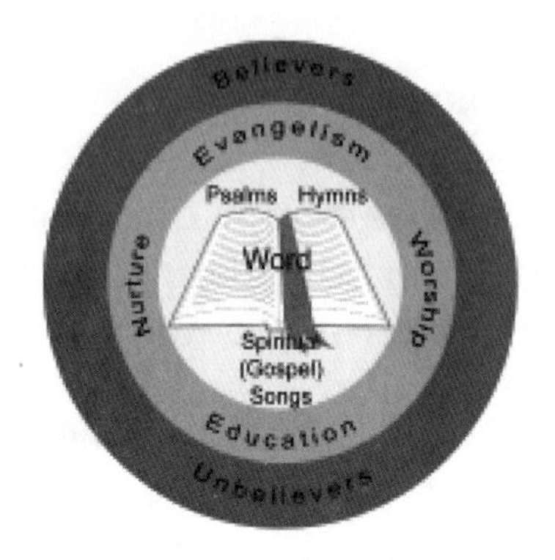

Looking at the illustration for a moment and examining its implications, one can clearly see that the Word of God is at the center of everything one does. All music for the church and the believer's life should derive from the foundation of the Word. Questions such as, Is this a good song? Is this music a Christian can listen to? Is this an appropriate song for this aspect of ministry? are all questions that should be answered from the perspective of Scripture.

From the centrality of the Word, the discussion now moves to the types of music that can be used powerfully and appropriately to declare the Word. The music may be from psalms or it might also be a hymn. Another option is the gospel song or spiritual song. Use of the various types and texts allows for great musical diversity and freedom.

All types of music should be used or related to the four primary areas of ministry: the ministry of worship, the ministry of education, the ministry of evangelism, and the ministry of nurture. Through these organized ministries, there are opportunities for a wide range of musical expression. Christian music belongs in the church as well as in the home, the mall, the concert hall, and the sports arena. Music belongs outside the church as well, providing opportunity for choirs, vocal and instrumental ensembles, and so forth to go into the community and minister in several different venues. Concerts in the mall, the market place, the athletic facility, the nursing home or at the local television or radio station provide excellent opportunities for music ministry. Music has a powerful delivery system for sending the Word into the world.

Essential Elements of Performance and Style

It is important to understand that the emphasis of all aspects of the music ministry advocated in this course is derived from Scripture. It is interesting to consider the questions: What do scriptures reveal concerning the manner of performance of music? and, How do singers and instrumentalists perform music in a Scripturally and Biblically correct manner? While Scripture is silent as to which musical styles are appropriate in worship, it does speak out regarding the manner or way believers sing and play in public worship.

The apostle Paul, well-known preacher, missionary, disciplinarian, and leader of the church, was also possibly one of the principal musicians of the early Christian church—apparently an accomplished musician. He even composed some of the early Christian songs in his writings. One such example can be found in Ephesians 5:14.[1] Paul wrote more about music and music performance than any of his peers.

In 1 Corinthians 14, Paul addressed the issue of tongues and interpretation of tongues. In verse 15, concerning the edification of the church through singing, and, by implication, in playing, he writes an answer to the question of order. "I will sing with the spirit, and I will sing with the understanding also." The *New International Version* renders verse 15 as follows: "So what shall I do? I will pray with my spirit, but I will also pray with my mind; I will sing with my spirit, but I will also sing with my mind." Here, Paul seems to be appealing for a manner of singing—an interpretive style of singing—that is founded on two basic and important concepts of musical performance in the worship service. These are distinctions that make Christian music, Pentecostal music, and worship music different from other forms of musical expression, such as classical, popular, country and rock. These important principles are as follows:

1. *Music should be performed in a spiritual and/or spirited manner.* Spirited singing calls for physical and emotional involvement and participation where the singer injects enthusiasm, personality, and musical interpretation into the performance or time of worship. This highly personalized involvement in

[1] For further reading, see bibliographic entries for Boschman (*Prophetic Song*), Reynolds, and Blomgren.

singing or playing music brings a new perspective. Paul also indicates in 1 Corinthians 14 that spiritual singing allows for the prompting, the direction, and the energizing of the Holy Spirit, whether in an individual, a praise group, a choir, or through the entire congregation. Even a praise band, instrumental ensemble, or a Christian orchestra can bring anointed music to the worship. It seems that Paul is saying, that worshipers not only come to the event with enthusiasm, but they can also be energized and touched by the power of the Holy Spirit as they perform.

> My desire is always to sing with the power and energy of the Holy Spirit. I have learned that my solo singing is much better and more powerful when I submit to the enabling power of the Holy Spirit. I have discovered that people tolerate and sometimes even enjoy my singing, since I no longer do it solely on my own. I bring everything I have, my whole self, to the experience and give it over to the anointing of the Holy Spirit. If I understand scriptures on this, we can then say that the Holy Spirit sings in the land today through believers. Not only does the Spirit sing, but the Spirit also plays prophetically through believers.

The Pentecostal tradition has always been one of fervent and enthusiastic singing and playing before the Lord.

2. *Music should be performed in a manner that is understandable and intelligible.* While it is desirable

to be involved physically and emotionally with the music, it is equally essential to be involved intellectually—to engage the mind as well as the emotions. Singing in the church will always be more effective when care is taken to ensure that the text of the song, along with its concepts, are readily heard and understood by the listener. Musical excellence—practicing, singing in tune, having ensemble—are also of spiritual value. It is spiritual to have skillful playing with the understanding that he "who sits in the seat of the scornful,"—the hearer of the music—can be touched.

It should be noted that song texts ought to always have a doctrinally sound and inspirational message. Musicians should be faithful in emphasizing pronunciation, ensemble, and technical proficiency, which are all desirable parts of the spiritual act of singing. When music is carefully selected and well prepared—both as to message and technique—and when it is anointed by the energizing touch of the Holy Spirit, it becomes a powerful force to change the lives of men and women.

In summary, there is no dichotomy between being spiritual and being excellent. Rather, there is a Scriptural model including both. The priestly and prophetic functions of music ministry need to be developed in the primary ministries of the church—worship, education, evangelism, and nurture. The manner of singing, therefore, suggests that believers sing with the Spirit to touch the emotions, and with the understanding to reach the mind.

5

A Worship Paradigm

It is important now to examine the underlying structure and organization of the worship service. An attempt will be made to develop a paradigm that is both Biblical and applicable to the 20th-century worship service. When the church comes together to worship, it is important to understand the Scriptural and cultural elements present that are pleasing to God and that minister to needs of both believers and nonbelievers. Music is an important means for presenting and expressing those elements.

Music and Worship

There are five important realities to consider when planning music for the worship service.

1. *Music reflects the people who are present in the service.* The kind of music performed will be a reflection of the people who are involved in attending a worship service in any given church.

2. *Music attracts the kind of people a church wants to reach.* Music transcends the boundaries of the church, reaching into the community and communicating with the people.

3. *Music encourages participation.* Response to music is typically more active than passive. It stimulates and promotes involvement. In a music therapy study, the research showed that even if people intended not to listen when music was present, they were still influenced by it. Further studies showed that when a person was placed in a soundproof room alone and when a particular kind of music was piped into the room for long periods of time, the person's body involuntarily responded to the music. Similarly, music in worship breaks down barriers and encourages people to join in and begin to worship the Lord.

4. *Music coordinates the elements of the service.* In the Old Testament, the playing of the shofar horn was used as a way of organizing the service. It was played to indicate to the people what was about to happen in worship. The shofar was also used in battle. In a similar fashion, leaders can use music to signal elements of the worship service.

5. *Music inspires worshipers to look to God.* Music has the compelling ability to bring worshipers toward God. A complete worship experience involves the cognitive—the learning and understanding processes. It involves the aesthetic—the feeling

and emotional processes. It also involves the psychomotor responses—the physical aspects of worship. Thus, music becomes an important part of each of these response types.

The Elements of Worship

In Pentecostal/Charismatic worship, emphasis has always been placed on freedom of expression, absence of formalism, and an atmosphere where the Holy Spirit draws the congregation into creative involvement. The Pentecostal tradition provides for a planned service while also allowing for creativity and freedom in worship. Within the framework of freedom, there must also be organization, structure, and design. To engage in corporate worship without structure is to ignore Scriptural principles and ideals. To have a service design and depend solely upon it leaves worshipers unable to be creative and respond to the power and the presence of the Holy Spirit. There is danger of losing meaning and effectiveness where little attention is given to prayerful planning.

Describing the function of the early church, Luke writes in Acts 2:42: "They devoted themselves to the Apostles' teaching and to the fellowship, to the breaking of bread and to prayer." Webber concludes that early Christian worship as described in Acts had two primary focuses—the teaching of the Word and the Table of the Lord.[1] With these two being primary, the pattern of worship in Scripture seems then to be fourfold: (1) the gathering, (2) the proclamation of the Word, (3) the thanksgiving, which also involves coming to the Table of the Lord, and (4) the dismissal—sending the people out for service. Furthermore, music can be used in each of these patterns of worship.

Patterns or structures of worship are variously described as liturgy, ritual or service order. The liturgy becomes the means of organizing and designing worship in a Biblical manner. Based on New Testament models, one presentation of the contemporary service follows this fourfold pattern.

The Gathering

The gathering takes place as the people prepare for worship. In the gathering, worshipers ascend into the presence of God through singing, celebrating, dancing, and sharing. Pentecostals usually organize this time into a three-phase design that is symbolic of temple worship (see Psalm 100).

[1] Robert E. Webber, *Planning Blended Worship* (Nashville: Abingdon Press, 1998), p. 21.

Transitioning to worship—the outer court

The first phase takes place as worshipers transition from the world into the presence of God—coming from the world with its hurt, its excitement, its joy, and its sadness. The gathering is a transition from that world into the world of the spiritual. This may be done in many ways. Pentecostals tend to organize this part of the service around singing and praising. They enter from outside through the gates of the temple into the temple itself, singing songs of high praise while preparing to enter into the presence of God. There is opportunity for involvement, not only musically but also physically and intellectually. There are many different and effective uses of music suitable for this time of worship. Recorded music, music videos, instrumental music and individual or group vocal performances can all be used in preparation for worship. The possibilities are infinite.

Entering into worship—the inner court

In the second phase, worshipers continue singing songs of praise and adoration as they move toward songs of humility and cleansing, experiencing the transcendent nature of God. Praise begins to become more intimate. It is now that the focus becomes more centered on God the Father, the Son and the Holy Spirit, and the worshipers' desire to worship God becomes more intense.

From that point, symbolically, (as it was done physically in the Old Testament) worshipers enter the temple. It is a symbolic transition, because now believers are the temples of God—the residence of

God himself—wherein dwells the Holy Spirit. Thus, Old Testament, literally, and New Testament, symbolically, are described in these stages and locations of worship.

Celebrating the presence—the Holy of Holies.

In this third stage, believers enter the very presence of God and begin to sing songs of confession and relationship. As they sing songs of fellowship with God, they move into the Holy of Holies—His presence. Worship becomes a spiritual experience as the believers worship Him in Spirit and in truth and allow their spirits to commune with His Spirit. When believers get to this place, it is an awesome moment. It is not easy to predict when such a moment will occur in a service, and these transitional elements do not always happen in the same order. While the stages and principles remain the same, one cannot depend on continuity and order alone—that is not sufficient. Worshipers also need to depend on the direction of the Holy Spirit to draw them even into the Holy of Holies.

> In my own experience, I have been in services where I've seen this happen at the beginning of the service. On other occasions, the entering into the Holy of Holies might come at the very end. Whether it is before or after the sermon or during the time of praise and worship, the important principle is that God's people experience His presence and enter into worship. The moment they are

> seeking, the time that is most vital and critical is then—the time when the people enter into the Holy of Holies.

Other contemporary patterns are expressed in four and even five phases of worship; likewise, music is a primary function in all of these approaches.

The Proclamation

The Word of God is the next focal point of the service. After gathering together in the presence of God and feeling His touch, believers are now ready to hear the Word and have it applied to their lives. Here believers experience the preaching and teaching of the Word. This is the opportunity for God's people to be disciplined, molded, and shaped by the power of God's Word. While the primary activity is the preaching and teaching ministry, music may also be used as a means of proclaiming God's Word.

The Thanksgiving

Here as individuals and as a congregation, God's people respond to the Word of God in thanksgiving. They may even take time to share their thanks with one another. This time of sharing thanks was common in the early Pentecostal churches just as it was in the New Testament church. Time is provided for members of the body to share testimonies of miracles in their lives, to tell each other about the blessings of the Lord, or to simply stand and give thanks to God. This is a good time, although not in every worship service, to come to the Table of the Lord and experience the blessings of a Communion service. Music can be used in many creative ways during this time at the Table of the Lord.

The Dismissal

It is during the time of dismissal that God's people consecrate themselves for the service of the Lord. They commit themselves to go out into the world to joyfully serve Him. Here is an opportunity to use music as a means of bringing people together. When people sing songs about giving themselves to the Lord, of dedicating their talents and abilities to Him, they can unite in consecration and commitment. Now the church is sent out joyfully for ministry. The people of God go forth in the benediction of the Father, the Son, and the Holy Spirit to serve God and do His will.

These four elements of worship exemplify a complete, Biblically based worship experience. The typical Pentecostal worship service usually contains some or all of the elements of worship previously discussed. The order of service is simply a way to organize and participate in worship, while at all times being creative and submissive to the will and flow of the Holy Spirit. There is great blessing in diversity. Even though these elements are mentioned in some easily understood order, there are no requirements that in every worship service all the elements unfold in exactly the same way. The actual order of the elements usually followed in the Pentecostal worship service will be discussed in the next chapter.

6

The Service Design

This chapter is devoted to the design and format of the elements comprising a typical Pentecostal worship service. When combined together into a complete service format, they become the order of worship or the liturgy. Again, these two essentials are emphasized: (1) It is important to plan well, and (2) After planning the service, the Holy Spirit should be invited to have control. Music leaders should then leave themselves open to the direction of the Holy Spirit.

Call to Worship

The first element, the prelude or the call to worship is the time of preparation for worship. It may feature music of any tempo or style, but usually the music is upbeat and celebratory. "Our God Is Lifted Up" is an example of a typical call to worship.

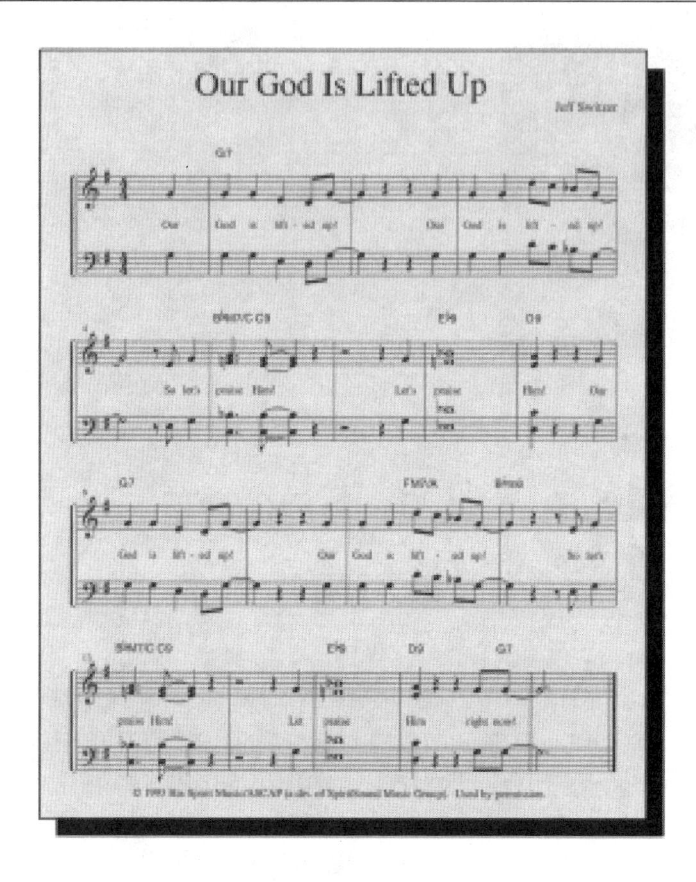

The text encourages the worshipers to lift up God and praise Him now. The next part of the song is a paraphrasing of several Scriptural passages about praise. The tempo is fast-paced and the manner of performance is spirited.

Praise and Worship

The next element is celebration or praise and worship. Congregational singing is usually the primary focus during this time. Pentecostals have always enjoyed worshiping in celebration, but have only recently called it praise and worship. They have also begun to distinguish and/or separate the two terms as to meaning and purpose. In praise and worship, the congregation is usually heavily involved in singing, being led by a worship leader and choir or praise group. The three-phase pattern is often used here.

The following three songs can be used to illustrate this three-phase concept.

The first example is "I Will Praise You." This is a jubilate or praise, expressed by a joyful affirmation of "I will praise You for as long as I live. I will lift You up." The text is positive and is sung in a spirited manner providing a way, as it were, for worshipers to leave the outer court and progress into the inner court.

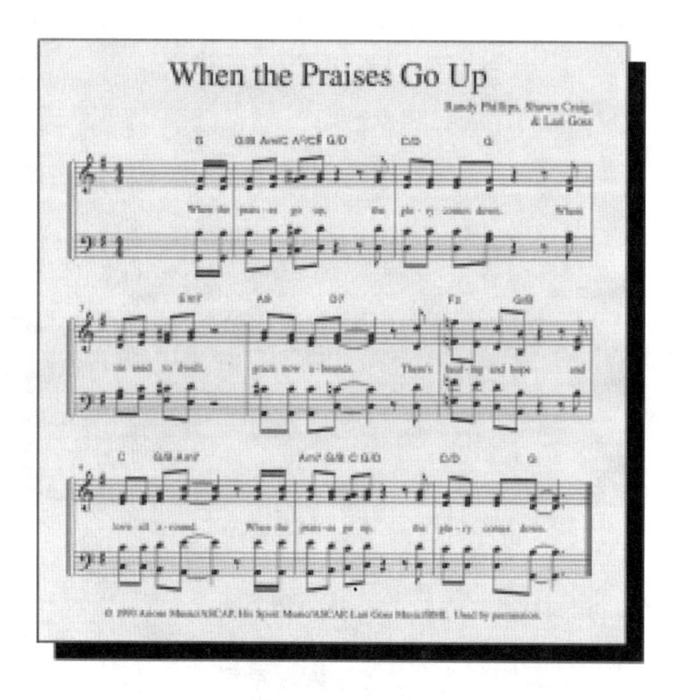

In the second example, the music tempo slows slightly while maintaining a positive feeling. The text proclaims "When the praises go up, the glory comes down." What a beautiful way to transition from the outer to the inner court. When worshipers think about sending up praises to God, then they experience His glory.

The praise and worship segment is concluded in a much more reflective and tender expression of adoration to the Lord, with the words, "I love You, Lord, and I lift my voice." This is almost a prayer that the Lord will find these words of praise beautiful and acceptable to His ears. Hopefully, the worshipers are now ready to enter the Holy of Holies and feel the warmth of His touch. This is why believers give Him their praise in love, worship and adoration.

The Reading of Scripture

Next, is the progression to the reading of Scripture. Music does not necessarily accompany this part of the service. However, the reading might be done in several different forms. The spoken and often responsively read Word is experienced during this time.

The Prayer

Often during the prayer, even though it may be done by an individual or in a congregational fashion, music of an instrumental variety is used to accompany this aspect of the service.

The Sharing

The sharing comes next in order. This time is usually a sharing of music that has been specially prepared by the skilled musicians of the church—soloists, instrumentalists, a small ensemble, or a choir. The following two examples of choral music might be used during the sharing.

The first example is for a choir and soloist. The text is presented in story form, recalling the healing work of Christ. "There's a Healer in the House" confirms the presence of the Lord and encourages worshipers to exercise their faith, for now is a time for blessing—a time to reach out and touch the Lord. The song is an excellent example of a gospel song being used to communicate a message of faith.

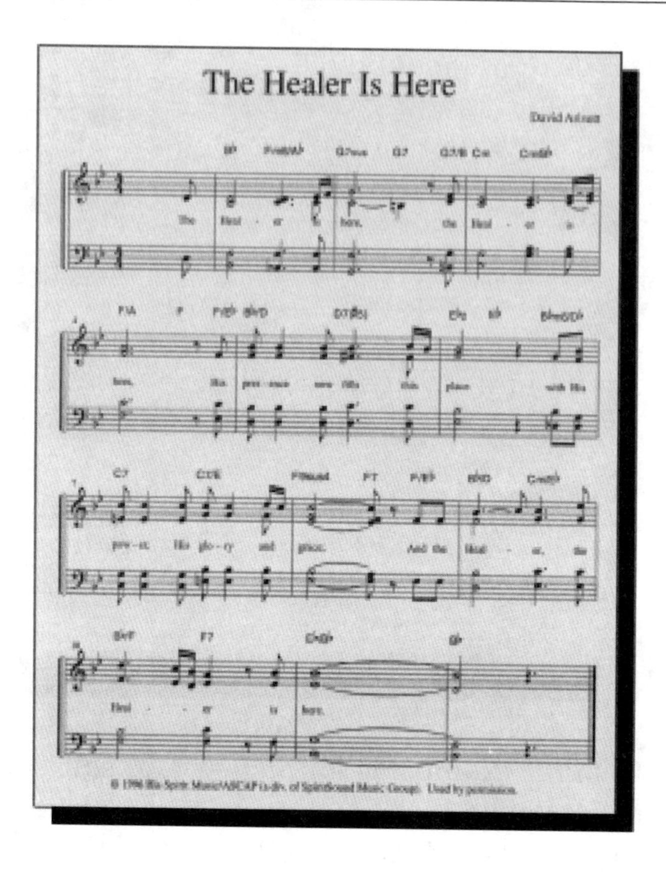

"The Healer is Here" is a contrast in style, but has the same positive witness. This contemporary chorus, with a bridge, is faith affirming in an entirely different manner. It simply confirms the presence of the healer, without making use of the more dramatic story-telling technique used in the previous example.

The Offering

Music will normally be presented by the pianist and organist or a small instrumental ensemble or the church orchestra during the offering. Styles and tempos may vary according to the objective of this aspect of worship. This can be a time for creative use of all the various instrumental soloists and ensembles of the congregation. The choir or other vocalists may also sing during the offertory.

The Sermon

The sermon may be preached or it may be taught. The music should emphasize the theme of the message and prepare the congregation for this high point in the service when the church is exhorted directly by the pastor or preacher.

The Invitation

The invitation is a time for forgiveness, consecration and commitment, bringing believers and sinners alike into the presence of God. During this time the people become aware of the opportunity for blessing and healing of the mind, body and spirit. They experience the touch of God. The music accompanying the invitation is usually reflective and moderate in tempo.

The Dismissal

The people of God are given a blessing or benediction. They are affirmed as believers. They are assured of the faithfulness and love of God, and they are sent forth into the world for the work of the Lord and to live the Christian life. There is cause for rejoicing and hope.

"We Have a Mission" and "We Give You Thanks" are two examples of music suitable for use at this time in the service.

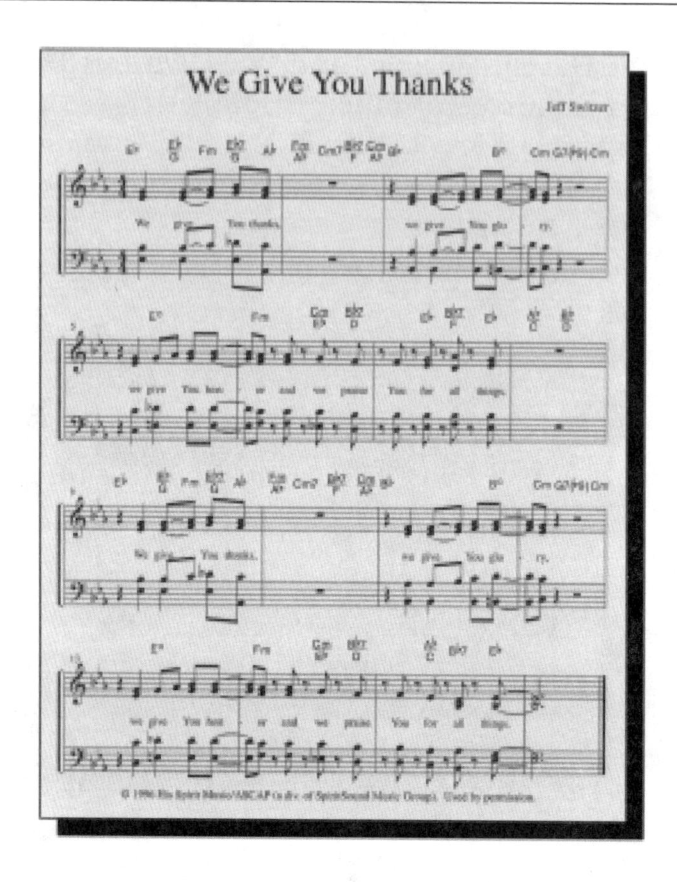

Both illustrate how the congregation might be sent out. The first example is a song of commitment, reminding believers of their responsibilities to go into the world, to go into the darkness, and to dispel the darkness with the light of the love of Jesus Christ. The second example is an exuberant expression of thanks for blessings received and for blessings to come. In both instances the congregation is dismissed in a positive and committed manner.

All of the service elements may not be present in every worship service, and they may not always occur in the same order, but they are representative of the typical Pentecostal design for worship. Service planners and leaders should always strive for creativity and variety while allowing for the direction of the Holy Spirit.

7

Blended Worship

In order to consider the responsibilities of developing an effective 21st-century Pentecostal worship service in a highly diverse culture, it is necessary to examine the idea of blended worship. The concept of blended worship is discussed in the context of the various service elements presented in the previous chapters. Blended worship and blended music attempt to bring the traditional and the contemporary together something old and something new, a previous generation sharing with present and future generations. This blending of the past and present allows for variety in the context of unity. It makes room for differing ethnicity, traditions, demographics, tastes, and musical styles, all reflecting the beautiful diversity of the family of God. This worldwide community of faith is a diverse culture made up of men and women of various races, traditions, tastes, and musical abilities, gathered together in preparation for that time when believers will truly be blended together in the presence of God and around His throne. The concept of blended worship is worthy of careful consideration of its value in the worship service.

Blended worship calls for balance. Balance is the key—balancing the times for worship with the time for the Word; balancing all forms of worship rather than limiting worship to one or two forms; balancing by allowing for the flow of worship versus a concrete, unchanging order of worship; balancing the worship in the Spirit and the worship in the understanding; and by the balancing of spontaneous worship with planned worship. Balance brings life. Balance creates freshness. If there were only one person in a particular church, it would be easy to select music that relates to that individual. A congregation having more than one person (or desiring to retain more people) needs to strive for blended music and musical styles in order that all can be involved and blessed.

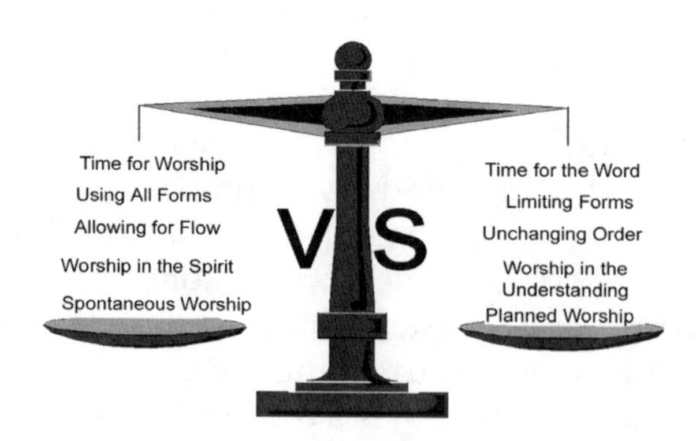

The Pentecostal worshiper who feels that there is no room for diversity of ideas, no room for the charismatic or the traditional in the kingdom of God must rethink how big God is. People cannot put God in a "worship lockbox." God uses all types of worship to advance His kingdom. Life displays an array of music; likewise, believers offer him an array of praise with a variety of music, reflecting a variety of worship forms. In order to understand the importance of blended music in worship, it might be helpful to examine various churches and their use of music in the context of worship.

Traditional Pentecostal Worship

In the worship service of the traditional Pentecostal church, 25 to 35 minutes of a 60- to 90-minute service may be devoted exclusively to music. The music usually is very enthusiastic and quite emotional. There will be applause throughout the service—applause to the music, applause to the blessings of the Lord, and applause to the sermon. Freedom and flexibility is built into the service and music assumes a role of importance.

Charismatic Worship

The distinctions between charismatic worship and the traditional Pentecostal worship begins with the use of music. In a charismatic church, 45 minutes to an hour may be devoted entirely to praise and worship through music. That is a significant amount of time for music. Also, in the typical charismatic service, there is a great deal of physical activity that may take place with the accompanying music, for example, jumping, swaying, dancing, waving banners, free and liberal applause—and, as in the Pentecostal service, liberal applause is sometimes accompanied by shouts of "Amen" and "Hallelujah." This opportunity to celebrate Christ and the joy of salvation in an exuberant manner will last at times until that point in the service where the Table of the Lord becomes central. The charismatic service concludes with time devoted to music.

Traditional Worship

Traditional worship, not only in the liturgical churches but also in the evangelical church, presents a more formal service order. Time reserved for music in the traditional/evangelical worship service is normally less than in the previously mentioned worship styles, lasting perhaps only 15 to 20 minutes. A call to worship, congregational singing, some choral music and a choral benediction are usually present. Emphasis is placed on the teaching and preaching aspects of the service. Usually, worship is more reserved and devotional, emphasizing the doctrines of the church as exemplified in the Biblical record rather than personal experiences and personal testimonies of the victorious Christian life.

Revival-Centered Worship

The revival-centered worshiping church is a relatively new phenomenon in the late 20th and early 21st centuries. A distinctive of the revival-centered church is that literally hours may be devoted to worship in a single service. The service may begin with as much as an hour of singing, referred to as praise and worship. The hour is spent standing, while singing, jumping, clapping, and praising the Lord. A worship leader, together with a praise team or choir leading the congregation in participation, controls this time of worship. The music is typically keyboard and rhythm-driven. Both music and worship can be typified by descriptions like fervent, enthusiastic, repetitive, joyful, and intense. Short teaching times are normally interspersed throughout the rather long service. There may also be, brief testimonies or exhortations with teaching about the Word, a doctrine, or a belief, which is then followed by more music or prayer. Almost without exception there is an invitation for worshipers to come to receive salvation, healing and blessings. Long seasons of prayer may occur during these times, and music is used as an accompanying element. Before the service is concluded, there may be another opportunity to worship through music.

Word-Centered Worship

In the word-centered church, time devoted to worship and singing tends to be very brief, more like the traditional service. There is some time for music, but most of the elements of the service point to the message. The message is more likely to consist of teaching than it is of preaching. Worshipers are encouraged bring their Bibles, notebooks, and study materials. Emphasis in the service is given to talking about the lesson of the day, the learning for the day, or the teaching for the day. The worshiper is strongly encouraged to take notes.

To summarize, probably not one of these traditions ought to be abandoned entirely for any of the others. Rather, the church needs to consider the merits of each and utilize all of them in a blended service of worship. Simply stated, do those things that are taught in Scripture, committing to come together around the Table of the Lord, and learn from Him to accept one another and appreciate each other's traditions and tastes. Above all, believers are joining hands to become equal partners in the family of God. When people are tempted to feel that their particular style of worship is better than the other person's, the result is spiritual pride. Proverbs 16:18 cautions that "Pride goes before destruction and a haughty spirit before a fall." Because God blesses worshipers in the style and form of worship they prefer, does not mean that He is blessing them exclusively. The community of faith makes room for brothers and sisters in Christ to approach Him in entirely different stylistic forms and still experience Him and be touched by His presence. This realization increases one's confidence in the faith and witness of fellow believers, and it removes the awesome responsibility of deciding for God who is part of His body and whose worship pleases Him most.

Thus, blended worship and blended music call for balance. A conscious attempt must be made to understand, accept and tolerate differences in styles, tastes, traditions and designs in order that worshipers may be blended together into a church that represents the entire family of God.

Modeling Blended Worship

In relation to the need for acceptance of diversity of styles and approaches in blended worship, it is appropriate to consider the process of modeling worship, as well as developing models for worship leaders. There are several principles to guide music leadership in this process. Effective modeling and leading in worship depend in large part on the following. (These same principles also apply to the evangelism, education and nurturing ministries of the church.)

1. *Developing relationships.* Relationship is based on personal connections, developing mutual love and positive regard for one another. Effective ministry and worship presentation can never be accomplished apart from teamwork based on mutual respect. Without doubt, the ability to develop and sustain nurturing relationships is the most important ingredient for success in ministry.

> In studies that I have done in my work with music ministers and music pastors, we have discovered that the number one ingredient of success for music ministers is the ability to get along with people—to build lasting relationships. The number one reason for failure, not only in music leadership but also in almost any form of service, is the inability to get along with others. So, I strongly emphasize that the

> most important aspect of a music minister's work revolves around coming to understand how to function on a team under the leadership of God's anointed—the senior pastor.

The leader of the team is the pastor. His authority and role are derived from Scripture, and he is responsible to provide leadership in all aspects of ministry. The music pastor or the worship leader then works with the pastor, and Biblically and spiritually, he works under the authority of the pastor in organizing and supervising the music ministry. He or she may then organize others on the team to assist them—praise teams, choirs, bands, orchestras, and various music ensembles. Each member of the team commits to supporting and uplifting one another as needs are met through ministry. At the pastor's direction, each member of the music ministry team learns and commits support to the philosophy, the mission, and the goals of the overall ministry. These understandings and commitments are then communicated and modeled to the congregation. Since people learn by what they see, hear, and feel, it is important when leaders come before the people in ministry that they see, hear and feel a united ministry team. Music ministers are as of the tribe of the Levites—the priests who minister to the needs of the congregation. It is, therefore, important that music ministers are seen as devoted to God and as worshipers. They should not only be seen as leaders, but also as participators and partakers of the blessings of the Lord both through music and the Word.

2. *Developing the right attitude.* The music leader and the music team must have an attitude of servanthood, of meeting needs, and of ministry to the body of Christ. Ministry is all about meeting the needs of people. It requires the development of an accepting attitude. This begins with understanding and accepting spiritual authority and oversight. An accepting attitude continues by affirming and recognizing the abilities of peers who may have talent in areas that the music leader may not have. Mutual respect allows one to celebrate their roles and appreciate their contributions to the work of the kingdom of God. If a leader can develop this attitude when working with choir members, praise teams, instrumentalists and congregations, it will likely encourage them to have an accepting, affirming view of the leader and his work. Only then do leaders begin to see people as Christ would see them—encouraging them when they do well, but also loving them when they are in error. The accepting attitude loves, and affirms people, as creations of God even in difficult times. This attitude requires looking past unlikable personality traits and, even in the face of conflict, proclaiming to those we serve: "I love you with the love of the Lord. I receive you as a coworker and valuable member of God's family."

Attributes Of Success

The successful musician must also work toward demonstration of spiritual traits and attributes as he develops and leads in ministry and in worship. Some of these attributes are presented below for consideration.

1. *The successful music leader will be spiritual in life and outlook.* The apostle Paul instructs above all else to "be filled with the Spirit." Understand that the music minister's role is not to dominate the service or dominate others, but to develop spiritual insights necessary to understanding the needs of the people and to respond accordingly.

2. *The spiritual musician must be sensitive.* That is a beautiful concept—to be aware of the needs, hurts, skills and abilities of others. Be sensitive to the times when there is a need to work hard, drive hard, and prepare for success. Be sensitive to the times when there is a need to slow down and relax in the presence of the Lord. Be sensitive to the times when there is hurt in the body. Be sensitive to the times when there is joy in the body. Be sensitive when it is time for warfare as opposed to worship. Demonstrate genuine care and understanding of the needs of others.

3. *The spiritual musician must have musical skill.* There is a need for the spiritual musician to emphasize the importance of becoming more skillful. The Biblical model for the minister of music, praise leader, choir member and instrumentalist is to work diligently in order to perform before the Lord. The successful music leader must possess musical skills, sing with a pleasing voice, sing in tune, and direct skillfully. In addition, the leader should demonstrate respect for competency and musical skills, as well as for spirituality. It is not possible to overemphasize the principle of bringing one's best to the Lord.

4. *The spiritual musician must be submissive.* This is an important concept to consider when discussing success for musicians and their roles as team members. Be submissive first to the will of God. It is a joy to understand the benefits of finding His desires for the music program on any given Sunday, or what He wants for the development of the worship program. Be submissive to the authority of the Word and the church. Be submissive to the leadership of the Holy Spirit. The prospects for success grow in proportion to the possession of these spiritual attributes.

There are additional attributes and skills that help determine the success of a spiritual music leader. Further examination reveals that the music leader must first possess a vision. The leader learns to dream and set goals. Where there is no vision, the music program does not grow. Second, the successful musician has good communication skills and has learned how to communicate effectively with the people. Third, the successful musician has a healthy self-respect. This may be a difficult area for some musicians and for ministers of music in particular. Typically, the minister of music has difficulty understanding that even though performance of music is intensely personal, people's negative reactions are most often to the music not the worth of the performer. In any musical performance, there will be some who react positively and others negatively. Criticism is an inherent part of music performance, so the musician must develop a healthy self-regard in order to accept this reality. When people criticize honest efforts, the leader must learn to receive that which is useful and understand that he is called of God to his ministry. God gave him these skills and abilities, and He requires only that they be used for His glory.

Remember that the mercy of the Lord endures forever. There will come an end to the criticism and difficult times. Music ministry is not just about performance; it is also about passion. It is not only talent, but it is also faithfulness. It is not just worship, but it is also warfare—spiritual warfare. It is not only having the joy of leading, but also the privilege of following.

Ministers and leaders need to understand both the priestly and prophetic roles they are expected to fulfill in a congregation. The priestly role is to serve the people of God in worship, training, nurture, and mission. Music ministers attempt to meet needs, both felt and expressed. The prophetic role is to share the good news of the Lord. The songs they lead tell of salvation, healing, and blessings, as well as foretell His glorious coming. At times, they serve as worshipers, and at other times, they fill their roles confidently as warriors.

8

Organization and Ministry

The ministry of music in the Pentecostal church is so dynamic that a constant review of leadership trends is desirable. Useful paradigms are constantly emerging, but they need to be moved from theoretical concepts of worship to the practical modeling of worship leadership. An examination of these models should begin with a look at the relationships and responsibilities of the two most important worship leaders in the church—the senior pastor and the minister of music.

The Senior Pastor and the Minister of Music

These are two very important leaders in ministry, but from the viewpoint of Scripture, the pastor has the principle responsibility to provide effective leadership to the church and its staff, including the music minister. The music pastor has a special calling to develop an effective music ministry under the auspices of the pastor. To form an effective team, these two have to agree on responsibility, relationship, and function, not only between themselves but also other members of the ministry team.

The role of the music pastor in relationship to the senior pastor is developed in consideration of the following observations.

1. *The music minister should give his admiration, appreciation, and respect to the senior pastor.* Whether the pastor and music minister are best friends or spend time together outside the ministry is not material. However, it is necessary to build an effective working relationship where the music pastor, without reluctance, gives respect to the pastor. One is not obligated to like everything about a person in order to give that person respect and admiration. From the perspective of career longevity, this is excellent advice. Such an observation is not an invitation to employ phony and insincere praise, but if the best the music pastor can muster is gratuitous praise, the prospect of a successful long-term tenure seems quite bleak.

Even though music ministers are working in a spiritual context, they should understand that, like themselves, pastors are fallible people and should not be held to a standard approaching perfection in all things. If one ascribes worth and appreciation to that person, cultivates the habit of saying good things, and develops a lifestyle of sincere praise, then good feelings emerge. When one adopts a lifestyle of praise, he begins to develop a positive view of life, people, and the church. When one lives a life that exalts and edifies God, it is no longer difficult to think good thoughts and edify the church, the pastor, the music program, and the musicians with whom one works. This attitude opens the way to excellence.

2. *The music minister should respect the professional ministerial skills of the pastor.* The style of the pastor might be very different from the style of the music minister, but one should not view these differences negatively, instead celebrate them and engage in the process of growth. In turn, the music minister will receive admiration and appreciation for his own abilities.

The music pastor has an opportunity to utilize the help of the senior pastor and let this help be a positive asset to his success. Seek the advice and counsel of the senior pastor in everything. If the pastor is saying good things about the music ministry and music pastor, that will aid in developing a leadership team, and it will also greatly help to cultivate the appreciation of the music team and the congregation.

> In my personal experience as a minister of music for many years, I have learned not only to admire and appreciate the pastor, but whenever possible to get him actively involved in building the music ministry. For example, I like to stand with the pastor as the congregation exits at the end of the service. This provides an

> excellent opportunity for the pastor to overhear people expressing appreciation for the music. That's affirming, uplifting, and edifying to me. Even more importantly, if the pastor is listening, he will also hear the affirmation, and it may aid his understanding and appreciation for the music ministry. He might not have any idea that these people have appreciation for music or respect for the music minister. A simple show of support often turns into unexpected blessing.

3. *The music pastor should utilize the pastor in service preparation.* Never go through service preparation without inviting the pastor to come in and share with the performing group. The pastor may do a brief devotional, discuss hurts and needs, allow for a brief praise session, and finally lead in prayer before entering the sanctuary for the ministry of worship. A wise music pastor does not depend entirely on his own abilities, but utilizes those who are over him in the Lord.

Personal Prerequisites for Music Ministry

The church has always engaged in spiritual warfare, but in these times, it seems that the Enemy, more than ever before, is attempting to confuse and frustrate the church through its music. It is understood that Satan is a skilled musician who uses music very effectively in influencing the thoughts, feelings and behaviors of the believer.

In addition to this warfare in the musical and spiritual realm, there is also danger of the music leader being negatively influenced by the amoral world of today. Musicians are subject to the same societal, family, and personal temptations that confront the nonbeliever. These are a reality even in church life; therefore, a good suggestion would be to set standards of conduct that require serious consideration.

1. *It is necessary that the minister of music live a moral life.* This becomes an essential ingredient of the music leader's lifestyle, so that both peers and those whom they lead can have faith and trust—faith in their leader's stance and trust in their leader's commitment to live an exemplary life.

2. *It is essential that ministers of music be sincere Christians.* There is no place for insincerity. Co-workers want to know that these leaders live genuine Christian lives for the glory of the Kingdom.

3. *It is helpful to develop an attitude of confidence and poise.* To be confident in who one is and what one's mission is radiates to those who are led. To be confident in one's ability to do the job well is just as important as having competent people to work with.

4. *It is desirable to develop a healthy sense of humor.* There are times when it is best to enjoy the failure or awkward moment or misguided word. Relax, enjoy and demonstrate appreciation for the humorous.

5. *It is appropriate to be concerned about personal grooming.* One does not have to be handsome or beautiful, but appropriate grooming is definitely a positive attribute. Musicians are normally highly visible when leading or performing; therefore, they

should present themselves in the best manner possible.

6. *It is essential to develop a commitment to cooperation.* What can be accomplished when everyone is pulling in the same direction is the essence of synergy—cooperative effort. This commitment means more than just learning to get along with one another; it means truly supporting the efforts of each team member when those efforts support the mission.

7. *It is important that the music leader be dependable.* There is a widespread impression that musicians tend to be undependable and last-minute geniuses in planning. It has been said that some musicians plan their service order as they are driving into the parking lot. Sometimes, it is even assumed that musicians are "no-shows" unless they are the center of attention.

When music leaders model worship—when they lead worship—they demonstrate their leadership abilities. People then come to understand that they are dependable, their word will be honored, and they will be responsible to the commitments they make. Thus, if leaders would be the kind of worship leader they ought to be, and model the kind of leadership they ought to model, then they will be continuously committed to improving themselves and their image. The spiritual leader should always be committed to attaining excellence. With this kind of attitude, comes a commitment to training and education, taking risks and trying new things, singing new arrangements and new songs, and attempting to keep abreast of new musical developments. Music leaders should always strive to bring their best to the Lord, and that means to have ongoing effective training programs.

The Demands of Music Ministry

The first area of qualities demanded for effective ministry relate to musical duties. This entails the supervision and coordination of all the various music ministries within the church. To supervise and coordinate does not necessarily mean leading those programs, but it does mean being able to find people with musical abilities and developing those talents to be used in the program. The people who are selected will determine how good the program can become. They too need to be committed and learn to assist the music leader in developing and evaluating the various music programs of the church.

Musical duties also include supervision of the functional aspects of supporting ministry. Purchase and care of music, tuning and upkeep of instruments, preparation and presentation of media support, maintenance and care of risers, robes, stands and lights are all responsibilities of the music minister.

The next area of concern is administrative duties. Much energy will be devoted to planning for the ministry activities of the week, planning for recruitment, planning for rehearsal, and planning for redirecting. Three vital points need to be emphasized here.

1. *Recruitment.* If the leader fails to recruit new personnel effectively, at some point the supply system fails and programs begin to diminish in

numbers and quality. The wise minister of music sees it as his or her administrative duty to continually be engaged in the process of planning, thinking, promoting, inviting, and encouraging new people to be a part of the musical program.

2. *Rehearsals.* The time spent in rehearsal with the various ensembles and groups presents the greatest opportunity to effectively mold and develop one's music ministry. Rehearsal time is some of the most important, if not the most important, musical time one will spend each week. Here is where musical standards are set and growth begins to occur. Rehearsals provide time to build relationships and to promote ministry ideas and commitments. Rehearsals should be so interesting and relevant that the musicians will want to attend. These should be times of refreshing, combined with hard work and achievement. Rehearsals should start and end on time. They should be a model, a microcosm, of everything that will ultimately occur in the performance or service. The rehearsal should become a preview, a "prehearsal," of what will take place in the sanctuary. Rehearsal is a time to grow both in  musical ability and spiritual sensitivity. If leaders are preparing the musicians to lead in the worship of God, why not also take time for worship in the rehearsal? If leaders are preparing music that will increase the faith of the believer, why not exercise faith in the rehearsal? If the singers are going to sing about the excitement of being Christians, why not be excitingly involved in the rehearsal? Rehearsals can be life-changing. Musicians are in the life-changing business through their efforts in music

ministry. Rehearsal is where it all begins. Use it to ensure success.

3. *Redirection.* This process involves getting in long-term relationships with people. The leader is not just a Sunday motivator or leader of worship; he is involved with the people he leads throughout the week, month, year, and even the seasons of life. One of the most powerful aspects of an effective music ministry is the teaching—the experiences shared, the rehearsing, the worship, the praying, the beliefs and mutual faith. Leaders come to redirect the lives of those they serve. In any given choir or congregation, there are people who are struggling, needing help and guidance. An important aspect of what they do is to learn how to influence, teach, motivate, and redirect the lives of those they serve in order that lives are changed and needs are met.

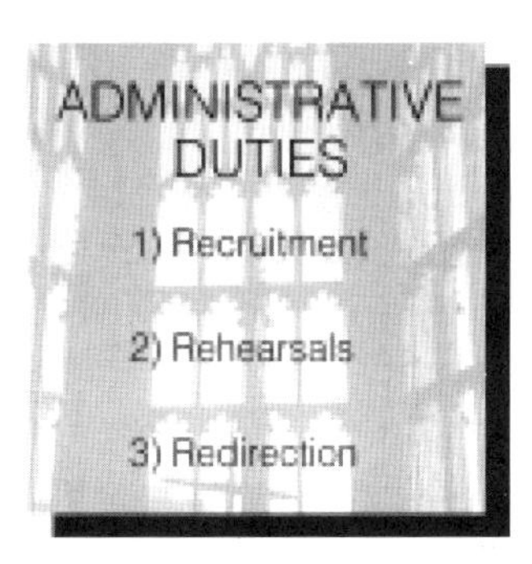

Spiritual Duties

A final area for discussion when considering leadership responsibilities is the area of spiritual duties of the music minister. Music ministry does not end with the final amen in the service. Responsibility does not end with the good-byes at the end of an invigorating rehearsal. There are spiritual duties in the church at large that become the responsibility of the music minister—being available for general church activities, being involved in outreach programs, assisting youth ministries or youth and Christian education ministries, being generally available and interested in doing a spiritual work.

> I think it was during my earliest job as a minister of music—a freshman in college, still a teenager—that I had my first opportunity to work with a loving, caring pastor. One of the things he said to me early in our relationship was, "I want you to be an effective musician, I want you to lead our choir, I want you to lead our worship, I want you to be really good, but I also want you to come to know our church." Little did I know that the way I would get to know him and the church would be to commit every Saturday to visitation of homes in the areas surrounding the church. I quickly learned how to do witnessing, how to promote church attendance and even how to recruit for the music program. At the end of a long exhausting day of visitation, we would always meet at a restaurant somewhere, and the pastor would graciously buy my dinner and then we would talk about what had happened. He would occasionally express to me some of his burdens and concerns and invite me to join him in prayer. Sometimes he would say, "Tonight before you

> go to sleep, don't remember just your ministry, but remember the church." When we would come together on Sunday morning, my view was different. I not only saw those people I worked with in music ministry, but I also saw the entire congregation and came to understand that it was my privilege to minister spiritually to them as well.

The church needs leaders with both musical and spiritual abilities who will commit to developing music ministry programs that will reach the needs of a diverse and changing constituency.

9

Expanding Methodology

The person who comes to worship today is perhaps more sophisticated than ever before. Today's worshiper has had exposure to different forms of visual and oral communications. Typical worshipers not only expect excellent music which is well performed, aurally stimulating and aesthetically pleasing, but they also expect the music to be accompanied with effective visual support. They have been exposed to television with creative lighting, drama, music, dance, graphics and other communication aids. They have likely experienced video and DVD visual and music formats. They may also be familiar with audio formats like CD, CD-R, DVD, ADAT, DAT, MIDI, Mini Disc, MP3 or cassette. These all impact the requirements and ingredients of the complete music and worship package to be considered for the church today. Dress, body language, verbal styles and movement are parts of the mix that will help determine the effectiveness of communication.

The Teaching Aspect

It will be helpful to consider pertinent methods and techniques that will contribute to successful ministry in music. Success in ministry includes calling, commitment, communication, and coordination. All of these can be effectively expressed through a continuous teaching process.

Teaching effectiveness

The first principle for consideration is teaching effectiveness. In every teaching setting, one should learn how to exercise the concept of economy of means. Leaders should not monopolize precious rehearsal or instruction time with sermonizing or excessive talking. This time is set aside for practice, study, devotion and sharing while preparing for ministry. The need is for teachers who can both discuss ideas and techniques cogently and demonstrate musical concepts aurally. The music minister should demonstrate what is musically desirable by singing or playing. The effectiveness of teaching is greatly increased when leaders illustrate through musical sound. Music is something that is to be experienced—it is to be heard and felt. Often music is described as being sound in time, thus teaching and rehearsing are made more effective by musical demonstration.

Teaching the whole

A second concept is teaching the whole (gestalt). Instead of attempting to teach music line by line or phrase by phrase, one should work toward developing an initial exposure of the entire composition or song. In teaching music, the leader should not make the mistake of taking one section or one part of the music and repeating it again and again. Rather, he should consider taking advantage of modern technology and show a video or play a recording of the complete musical performance as a means of introducing the music to the performers. The group should be allowed to listen to a CD or cassette version of the music to be learned. Then they should watch a video or DVD version of the music and techniques that the singers will be performing. This should be the first approach before breaking down into sectional rehearsals or before concentrating on learning individual notes or lines. This principle of teaching the whole ensures that the parts will be more easily learned and understood. With music, the power of the gestalt is in understanding and seeing how the message, the melodic, the harmonic, and the rhythmic all blend together. How does the harmonic structure relate to the melody? How does the text relate to the music? Consideration of these aspects results in developing an effective teaching and leaning approach. The conceptual or gestalt approach can improve and enliven rehearsals and, in the end, provide better musical results.

Using visual illustration

A third concept is to use visual illustration, both physical and emotional, in the process of communication. Music is physical, emotional, mental, and spiritual. To be able to illustrate these various aspects of life with visual examples is powerful. For example, when teaching communication skills in rehearsals and workshops, there are some fundamental attitudes and actions that will help increase the effectiveness of communication through music.

1. *The music can tell musicians and singers how to look.* When they are performing a happy piece, or one that has great energy or drive, it is desirable for the musicians, whether accompanists, singers, or soloists, somehow to look like the music sounds—or simply put, to visually convey the sound and style of the music. When the music is majestic, they should physically look majestic. If the music is smooth and relaxed, they should allow the body, eyes, and facial expressions to be smooth and relaxed. When the music is highly energetic, they should be energetic. If the music is sad, they should convey that look as well.

In a spiritual context, one should consider a performance attitude of sacred music that is based on Scriptural indications of musical performance by the Trinity—God the Father, Son and Holy Spirit. First, the singers should sing like God sings. In Zephaniah, God sings with joy over His people. When they sing joyfully and skillfully before the Lord, it becomes a powerful medium to change people's lives.

Second, the singers should sing with the attitude of Christ. In both Matthew and Mark, at the close of the Last Supper when Christ was about to go into the Garden with His disciples to begin His most difficult time in life, they sang a hymn. Part of this hymn is believed to contain these words from Psalms 115–118: "The Lord is good. His mercy is everlasting. The Lord is good. His mercy endures forever." If when facing His greatest challenge Christ could sing so gracefully, then surely singers too can sing beautifully and with conviction in every condition. In all times and circumstances, one should sing with the attitude of Christ.

Third, singers should sing with the inspiration of the Holy Spirit. When they perform with the enabling power of the Holy Spirit, it is better than anything they could imagine doing on their own.

2. *The words should tell the singers how to feel.* Sometimes musicians sing as if there is no power or life in the words; in fact, it would seem the music and the words do not go together. Words are sung and concepts are presented, but the musicians portray something entirely different. They should allow the meaning and the power of the words to influence not only what they say but also how they feel. It is important that both performers and listeners understand and feel the power of the text.

3. *The Holy Spirit, if allowed, will energize the music.* Musicians and singers alike should commit themselves to spiritual musical performance, energized by the Spirit. They should learn what it is like to minister in the spiritual realm, as well as in the intellectual and emotional realms. All that is needed

is to invite the Holy Spirit to come and participate in the singing and playing done unto the Lord.

The Musical Aspect

Both physical and emotional illustrations can be found in other instances. For example, when the music minister is teaching a group or an individual to perform music in a legato style, he should consider demonstrating, either verbally or physically, what is meant by legato. The word *legato* means "smooth, and connected music." To demonstrate disconnected or accented music, one should use the word *staccato*, or separated. The music minister can use such simple techniques as saying, "Let's do this in legato (smoothly); let's connect the music." Or he could say, "Let's do this in staccato (accented fashion); let's separate the notes."

If one is leading a congregation in singing the chorus, "I love You, Lord, and I lift my voice," the movements are going to be smooth, connected and flowing in order to indicate both the musical and textual sense of the music. By contrast, if one is singing about going to the Enemy's camp and taking back what has been stolen, then the movements will become separated and even militaristic in look and style. The worshipers will become very energized.

Believers demonstrate their belief in worship by becoming worshipers. Likewise, music leaders can demonstrate musical concepts by what they do physically, emotionally, and intellectually. They should develop a respect for the advantages that come from illustrating techniques, rather than simply talking about them. When talking about the placement of sound, the leader can give a visual demonstration of what to do. When talking about vocal projection, one can demonstrate the technique (preferably in the context of the music that is being learned) that will allow the sound to be projected with beauty and power.

Utilizing All Available Resources

Leaders should encourage their musicians to purchase recordings of the music they will be learning. When they are listening to the music they will be performing, they save valuable rehearsal time. When they are listening, they are learning, not only notes, but also style and feeling. They are becoming acquainted with the music even before they start to rehearse it. There is another powerful benefit from listening to tapes and CDs and watching videos—the listener is receiving ministry for their spiritual needs.

The use of sound tracks of prerecorded music to assist in learning and performing music is another useful tool for both singers and instrumentalists. A relatively new phenomenon is the development of split tracks. A *split track* is a musical device (CD, CASS or DVD) that is formatted to play instrumental sounds on the left side (of a two-track format) and vocal sounds on the right side. It makes it possible to hear the music with both sides blended together, and it also allows the listener to hear only instruments or vocals. By changing the balance control on the cassette player or the CD player, one can move the signal to the left side of the track and hear only instruments. Rehearsing with the track saves time, promotes ensemble, and aids understanding stylistic demands.

Playing along with the track is also a way to assist the accompanist in learning new chord patterns and new rhythms. It has the same advantage for singers. When the balance control is moved from straight up to the extreme right, they will hear only voices. In this manner, vocalists can hear their parts featured and improve accuracy, both musically and vocally. At some point, the music minister can bring everybody together and, through the marvel of technology, either perform with the accompaniment of the track or perform the music entirely live.

Music ministers should be encouraged. They can be bold and let inventive ideas and music technology become their friends. They can use them to develop excellence in all aspects of music ministry. They should not hesitate, but be willing to experiment and move toward the future. As one's music ministry develops, it can be improved technically, musically, and spiritually, all for the glory of God and the advancement of His Kingdom.

10

Music Support Systems

Several issues which relate to support systems, equipment, legal and ethical concerns need to be addressed. New developments in technology, ministry models, and legal issues relating to intellectual property and copyright matters are areas requiring the attention and understanding of the local church as it engages in ministry in an increasingly complex society.

Soundtracks

The use of soundtracks in music ministry, which support both teaching and worship, represents a significant step forward in enhancing church music. Tapes, CDs, DVDs, DATs and videos are effective tools for demonstrating singing skills, providing musical models for the individual or group, and upgrading the quality of the music program. Use of soundtracks and MIDI files with instrumentalists is also becoming more accepted. This potential for improving performance quality when working with volunteer musicians cannot be overemphasized. Singing with soundtracks in a church where there is no orchestra or accomplished musicians, or using soundtracks for a special event or musical drama, can be an invaluable addition to the impact of music and worship.

I remember a pastor calling me to come to his church to do a music workshop on a Sunday afternoon and lead the music in a special Sunday night program. Upon arriving and meeting the pastor, I suggested that to prepare for the seminar, I needed to get together with the pianist to look at some of the music we were going to do. The pastor said, "Oh, I'm sorry. The pianist called me about 30 minutes ago, and she will not be coming to the service today." I responded, "That's okay. I'll just meet with the organist then." And he said to me, "I hate to tell you this, but our organist resigned last month, and we do not have anybody to play the organ." When I then inquired about what we were going to do for music, he said, "What are we going to do? Why do you think I invited you to come here today?" So, I did what any resourceful music minister would do. I went to the car, found one of my daughter's jam boxes, brought it in, set it on the pulpit and selected some split tracks from the folio I always carry with me. When the choir came (to my surprise, only four ladies and one man), I began to work with them, utilizing tracks. We talked about singing techniques and worship, and rehearsed four or five songs to sing along with the tracks as we prepared for the service. When it was time for the "choir" to sing, I placed a mike in front of the jam box, turned on the track, and we began to sing. These were good singers with wonderful hearts, and before long, the Spirit of the Lord came down, and a beautiful service ended with people coming to the altar to receive blessings. At the end of the service, the pastor came to me and said, "I sure am glad you came today. The music was anointed, and it seems like our choir has already grown." I contemplated his comment for a moment, and looking at the numbers, I thought, *You are absolutely right. You have grown. When I came, there were only five, but tonight they grew to six.* Don't be afraid of the numbers. Think about the opportunity to take people where they are and move them to where you'd like for them to be. Use all the aids and resources available for the glory of God.

Displaying the Text

A phenomenon that is occurring in Pentecostal/ Charismatic churches throughout the world is the seeming abandonment of the traditional way of providing texts for congregational music. For centuries, the church has placed a hymn book or a songbook in the hands of the congregation to use as they sang. Now, another method, sometimes referred to as singing off the wall, has come into vogue. If not off the wall, a screen is displayed, and instead of reading the words from a hymnal, song sheet, or bulletin, the words are projected onto a white surface. This method allows the congregation to easily see the words and at the same time be free to raise their hands, clap their hands, or engage in other physical movements while singing.

While this development certainly has its merits, one should not totally do away with hymn books and gospel songbooks. Furthermore, one should not totally abandon the practice of printing the words of praise choruses and hymns in the bulletin. The intent is to encourage the use of blended media in support of blended worship. The appropriate use of slides, overheads, and PowerPoint presentations with congregational singing is desirable and represents technological advances that can enhance the worship experience.

Another thought should be taken into consideration. When enjoying the currently popular trends in church music, one should remember that what seems old was once the popular trend. This suggests that what is "in" now, may be "out" tomorrow. There are texts and tunes from every era that should never be lost. The best way to preserve the worship music throughout decades and centuries is to print it in book form for present and future generations.

Sound Reinforcement

The discrete use of sound reinforcement can enhance worship as much as any of the technological support systems available. While the purpose here is not one of presenting a detailed technical discussion of sound, the advantages and disadvantages of good and bad sound are worthy of note. Since everything in today's Pentecostal/Charismatic service is sound reinforced, its importance cannot be overstated. If the singing is to be effective, it must be heard. If the message from the Word is to be understood, it must be heard. This society is accustomed to, and demands, well-designed sound reinforcement. Good sound begins with an adequate system and adequate power for that system. A soundboard must be carefully chosen. It should be free from noise, and when there are technological problems, someone who understands sound must be available to remedy the problem. The pastor and musicians need a monitoring system so they can hear the sounds they produce. It is desirable to provide adequate monitor coverage for each of these areas: pulpit, choir, praise group, and band or accompanists.

Microphones

In the worship setting, different types of microphones are needed for different musical and vocal demands. This is one of the areas where the sound program may experience problems. It is necessary to understand that the types of microphones used for the band may be very different from those for the soloists, praise team, or choir. There is also a need for teaching proper use of each type. This is almost always a sensitive area for both sound technicians and volunteer musicians.

The choice of microphone, of course, depends on its intended use. For speaking, solo singing, or praise groups, a unidirectional microphone is usually preferred. This is the typical type microphone that is used by speakers and soloists. As the name *unidirectional* implies, the microphone receives the sound primarily from a single direction. Obviously, this is not the type of microphone best suited to capture the sound of an orchestra or choir. Since the microphone is unidirectional, the quality of sound and range of dynamics is best when one speaks or sings directly into it. Holding the microphone below the face, to the side, or singing over the top of it will result in a dilution of sound qualities.

Instruction in the proper use of the microphone will measurably improve results.

Another type of microphone, primarily used for larger groups, is the omnidirectional or multidirectional microphone. This microphone has a much larger field for reception of sound. This greater area makes it possible to use two or more of these microphones, properly placed, to successfully capture the sound of the full choir or orchestra.

Sound team

Members of the sound team should be made to feel that they are a vital part of the church. They are not just much needed technical assistance, but they are also part of the ministry of the church—particularly the music ministry. There ought to be opportunities for regular sessions devoted to discussing—from a team perspective—sound, lighting, and drama with the music personnel and the pastoral staff.

Drama and Movement

Drama is becoming increasingly important in worship and in other public services of the church. Varied styles and approaches are used in order to include dramatic elements. For instance, the call to worship might be a youth group doing a dramatic presentation often accompanied by music. Some pastors are using illustrated sermons, including times for dramatic action to illustrate a sermon point. Occasionally, entire segments of the sermon may involve dramatic presentations. These presentations add a visual dynamic to the message.

Movement has also become an ingredient of the worship service. Dance, mime, human videos and other forms of sacred movement are increasingly used as an expression of worship. Each of these forms may be presented with musical accompaniment.

Multimedia

Multimedia productions have become an exciting innovation in the worship experience of the 21st-century church. Music, film, video, lights, and drama are all blended together in a dramatic expression of worship. The choir may sing while a video, mime, film clip or dance is presented, interpreting or reinforcing the message. The sermon may be interrupted by a film or video clip that dramatically empowers the impact of the message. Musical segments can be presented during the sermon. The use of live action and human tableau, can be used to illustrate the sung or spoken concepts. These are effective aids that need to be considered for use in the worship service. The larger church may have greater resources to support multimedia presentations, but the smaller church can be involved in using a variety of these resources as well.

Legal Issues in Music

Increasingly, the church is coming to realize that it has an ever-widening degree of ethical and legal responsibilities in many areas of ministry. Two practices by many churches that fall into the area of legal and ethical responsibility deserve attention and remedy. The practice of illegally copying music (copying without proper permission) and the practice of illegally recording music (recording music for sale without proper permission) are issues needing review and responsible action.

> I was invited to a church as the speaker for the Sunday morning worship service. When I entered the sanctuary, the pastor invited me to sit with him on the platform during the worship period preceding the sermon. As the singing began, he invited the congregation to reach into the pew rack and take out "our" chorus book. As I looked in "their" chorus book, to my surprise, I discovered that 150 pages had been duplicated on a copy machine and more than 300 worshipers were using this copied book. I could scarcely believe my eyes when I examined the inside cover and found these words: "Warning: It is illegal to copy this book. Do not photocopy." I was even more disturbed to discover that the illegally copied book was a publication of my own denomination.

It is illegal to copy printed music for the congregation, choir, orchestra, praise band or soloist in any form without permission of the owner of the copyright. To understand if and how music can be copied legally, it is important to have some knowledge of copyright laws. It is vital that the church act properly and responsibly in view of the fact that the law provides for a monetary fine or penalty for each copyright violation.

Why does copyright law provide penalties when music is copied illegally? It is because the law is protecting "intellectual property." It seems easy to understand the importance of protecting "real property," but when talking about protecting ideas, concepts, words, and melodies, the issue tends to blur. When people take things that do not belong to them, they are stealing, and that becomes not only a legal issue, but also a moral one. If someone takes a car that does not belong to him and does so without authorization of its owner, then he is stealing real property. If individuals copy music that does not belong to them, and they do so without authorization of the owner, then they are stealing intellectual property. Both actions are violations of the law. In creating music, money is spent writing, arranging, printing, and recording the music. Thus, not only is the writer of Christian music involved in the creation of music, but others also make their living by editing, arranging, orchestrating, printing, recording, and producing music for the believer. These individuals depend on the sales of music for their livelihood. When churches purchase music or pay for permission to use it, they are sustaining the Christian music community and keeping it viable. This is not just a legal issue, but it is also a moral and an ethical responsibility to one another.

Copy permission

It is possible to copy music, but it can be done only by permission of the copyright holder. There are at least three ways to obtain permission to use copyrighted material. First, purchase the music. If one buys the music, he is, technically, using copied music, but it is copied music that one has legally purchased. Second, in the absence of funds to buy the music, it is possible to obtain permission to use copied music by calling or writing the publisher and asking for permission to copy. Third, and generally the most convenient way, is to obtain a blanket license from a music licensing agency. This license or permission is issued on the behalf of the writer or publisher and provides copy permission only for certain circumstances. Permission to copy usually applies to "words only" for use in bulletins, song folios, slides, overheads, and PowerPoint presentations.

For this limited copy permission and in instances where a church does not have funds to purchase the music, they should consider using a licensing service supported by the Church Music Publishers Association. This licensing service is available to churches, schools, and groups in America and many other countries around the world. Christian Copyright Licensing, Inc., or CCLI, provides a blanket license for many church activities, including permission to copy music for congregational purposes. It also issues mechanical licenses for churches and groups to record songs by either audio or audiovisual means. On the behalf of publishers and copyright owners, CCLI can grant permission to put words only in bulletins, words only in chorus books, and display words only on the screen, either by slides or any other method of projection. These services are provided for an annual fee based on the size of the church. The very small church with limited resources pays minimal fees, while the larger church is assessed accordingly.

Periodically, CCLI will contact the member church for the purpose of surveying music actually used in its various ministries. The survey asks for information concerning all music that was performed, recorded, videoed or televised during the licensing period. It will seek information about the types of usage of all copyrighted music. This information is included in a database that will eventually determine payment of royalties to publishers and writers. Royalty amounts are determined by a weighting system that is based on the size of the reporting church and the number of performances. This licensing approach seems to be an excellent way for a local church to responsibly engage in music ministry and, at the same time, properly satisfy the copy and performance requirements of the law. It deals with the illegality issue and satisfactorily removes culpability from the local church. The CCLI approach can also provide an administrative function that saves valuable time and effort on the part of the church music staff. The music minister should remember that this copy permission applies only to congregational music. *It does not cover printed music for choir, orchestra, or vocal and instrumental ensembles.*

In addition to the matter of responsible use of printed music, the rapidly developing practice of recording church services or special performances is of growing concern as it relates to protection of the rights of music writers and publishers. While it may be desirable from a ministry perspective to record (audio and video) services and events, it is also desirable to responsibly satisfy the law as it relates to the recording and sale of copyrighted material. When a church group or soloist records copyrighted music in any medium, and that music is sold, the church assumes a legal and ethical responsibility to pay mechanical royalties for its use. Synchronization royalties may also apply to music performed for televised services or events. Simply stated, if a church records a service with music included, and parishioners purchase those recordings, the church is obligated to pay royalties, either mechanical or synchronizational.

A similar issue is that of the church recording its services or special events and making them available for television—local, regional or national. The church is then encountering another legal responsibility regarding the music performed. A synchronization right may be involved. Making recordings for sale—either sound or video—of the praise team, choir, band and orchestra is a powerful way to communicate the gospel and the mission of the church to the entire community. When these recordings are covered by prevailing laws, they also demonstrate concern for the total Christian community.

Churches should be open to using all of these technologies and support systems. However, they should make sure that they obtain the approval and support that will provide them with assurance that the ethical and legal responsibilities are met in all copying, performances, recordings, distributions, and sales of the music created. The power of music and the arts can be enhanced, preserved and presented to a world desperate for God through the use of contemporary technology and support systems.

11

Leading Worship

The ability to lead people in worship is central to the success of a music minister in most Pentecostal/ Charismatic churches. Often, the effectiveness of the ministry and personal contribution of the music minister is measured by success and competence in developing skills in leading worship. This increasing demand for skilled worship leaders in the contemporary church is reminiscent of certain aspects of the role and function of musical leadership in the Temple. This chapter will discuss several spiritual and musical behaviors necessary to becoming a successful worship leader.

Personal Prayer

Developing ability to lead in worship begins with setting aside regular time for personal prayer and devotion. The worship leader must be a worshiper. There can be no substitute for spending time alone in the presence of God—experiencing His touch, discovering His will, seeking His direction. In busy times of rehearsal, program preparation, and ministry activity, one should be careful to maintain a commitment to the spiritual perspective. Spiritual authenticity depends on the amount of time spent in study of the Word, personal prayer, and intimate worship. To be real, to be relational, and to be capable of leading worshipers into the presence of God demands a life committed to the importance of consistent prayer.

Developing a Plan

Failure to plan for worship and dependence on the creative and spontaneous aspects of worship may result in depending on meaningless repetitions of certain behaviors and failure to provide for the complete worship experience depicted in Isaiah 6. One way to assure that meaningful worship can occur is to develop a plan for it and then depend on the direction of the Holy Spirit to inspire creativity while bringing God's people into His presence. One should develop times in the weekly schedule to think about a worship plan, reflect on the various service elements needed, and plan the specific music experiences and songs that will be used. Additional issues that need to be considered are the following:

1. What songs will be used in the gathering or "praise and worship" segment?

2. What music will be used for the prayer response, the altar response, and the dismissal?
3. Who will be involved in the music presentations?
4. Have the musicians received adequate contact and given time for preparation?

One can ensure that the service will have a meaningful purpose and result by prayerfully and intentionally developing a plan. God will honor this approach and give results pleasing to Him.

Visualizing Results

Music ministers should begin to see or visualize how the service will unfold. They should also consider how people will respond and become involved in the service. Furthermore, they should determine whether there is variety in the music and whether it differs from that used in recent services. If leaders always use the praise group, choir, and featured soloists in the same sequence, performing essentially the same musical style, effectiveness is diminished. If leaders always transition from fast tempo to medium to slow and constantly repeat familiar songs without any creativity or variety, the congregation will be tempted to react passively, both mentally and emotionally. Music ministers should also think about change and variety within the constant of the typical service order. They should visualize the change and how it will affect the congregation while providing opportunity for blessings and realized needs.

Music-Directing Techniques

The successful worship leader must develop effective physical and verbal abilities that will provide meaningful direction of the musical responses of both performers and congregation. It is reasonable to expect a level of competence in the directing of music and commitment to excellence in all that is attempted in the service of God.

The visual aspect

People usually communicate with others visually even before they have opportunity to communicate verbally or musically. Many feelings and attitudes are shown initially by facial expression and body language. Leaders should be careful to look directly at the people they are attempting to lead. They should reach out to them, and demonstrate by facial expressions and body movements, how they want them to perform and respond musically.

If music ministers have already prepared for worship in personal prayer, there is no need to effect a spirituality with closed eyes and pained expression. Their primary role is direction and communication that results in leading worshipers into the presence of God. They should be a worshiper, as well as a leader of worshipers. Leaders should not totally remove themselves from this awesome responsibility. Negative congregational results often occur when the worship leader spends significant time with eyes closed in personal worship, or when the praise group gets caught up in personal blessings to the point of even ignoring others present. During these occasions, the congregation may be tempted to lose all sense of connection and involvement. The point is that worship leaders have the responsibility of modeling, both visually and verbally, the various aspects of the worship experience.

THE PHYSICAL ASPECT

Worship leaders need to learn what is acceptable in conducting technique. They need to know what is required physically in order to assure good musical direction. They need to be aware of what should happen in the use of body, hands, and eyes.

First, one should assume a posture where the feet are firmly planted and separated by approximately 10 to 15 inches. One foot may be slightly in front of the other, creating a look of comfort and confidence. They should relax the head and face, conveying attitude and emotion, and look directly at the people when talking to them or leading them in musical response.

Second, worship leaders should learn how to use signals and movement, primarily with the hands, that will allow them to initialize, continue, and conclude the performance of a musical thought, a complete song, or a musical composition. Technique is relevant to results.

Third, music ministers need to know how to promote good communication in order to assure better musical performance. In the matter of initiating sound, leaders should not depend on the accompanist or orchestra; this is the role of the leader himself. One must break through the silence and cause sound to be heard. When ready to begin the music, simply lift the hand. This is a universal sign, both musically and nonmusically. If someone raises his or her hand, it means stop and give attention. In leading music or worship, the leader begins by lifting the hand and gaining attention. When one has completely stopped the motion of the hand, that will indicate that something in about to occur—to talk or sing. Leaders can practice this in front of a mirror. They should bring their hand slightly up to get attention. If this is done while taking a breath, the congregation or performers will respond by also breathing. The technical term for this slight motion of preparation is *anacrusis*. After this preparation, the leader begins the music with a downward motion (the downbeat). The leader is illustrating style and tempo of the music by the manner and speed of the movement of the hands. A smooth and connected movement executed at a moderate pace indicates the music is being performed in a legato style at a moderate speed. Quick and accented movement indicates a fast tempo, performed in an accented or marcato manner. This is a simple approach that a pastor or music leader can use to develop better congregational and group singing. After starting the music, keep the hands moving until it is time to stop the sound. To indicate cessation of sound (cut off), simply stop the movement of the hands.

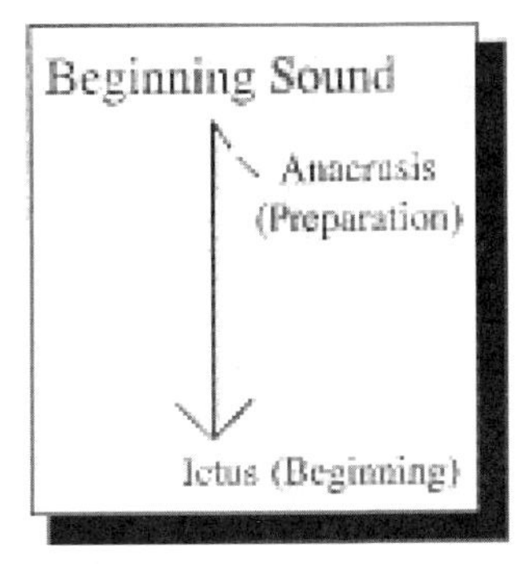

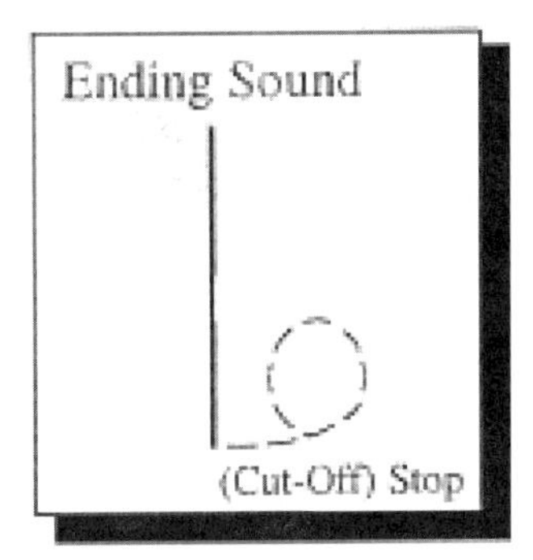

Three basic patterns are generally used to show the meter and rhythmic flow of the music. The first of these patterns is duple or two-part. Duple meter is analogous to the basic rhythm of life. Night is followed by day; rest is followed by activity. Youth is followed by old age; life is followed by death. This basic rhythm of life can perhaps be best understood by examining the heartbeat. It is two-part. The heart contracts to bring blood in, and it relaxes to allow the blood to flow out. Its rhythm is a period of stress followed by a period of relaxation. Many of the songs that are used in worship can be directed by using a duple motion or pattern.

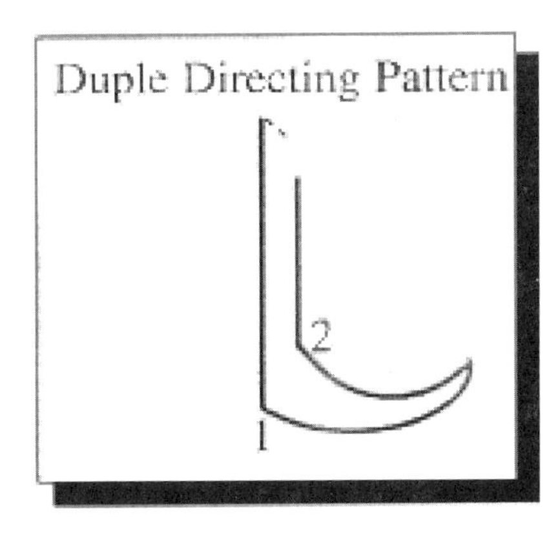

There are two motions of the hand for duple—down and up (toward the floor and toward the ceiling). The speed and movement of the hands determine tempo and style. This is not meant to be a detailed discussion of conducting technique, rather these suggestions are offered as practical aids for developing some competence in leading worship.

The next basic meter is triple or three-part. This meter requires a pattern consisting of three motions—down, right and up (floor, wall, ceiling).

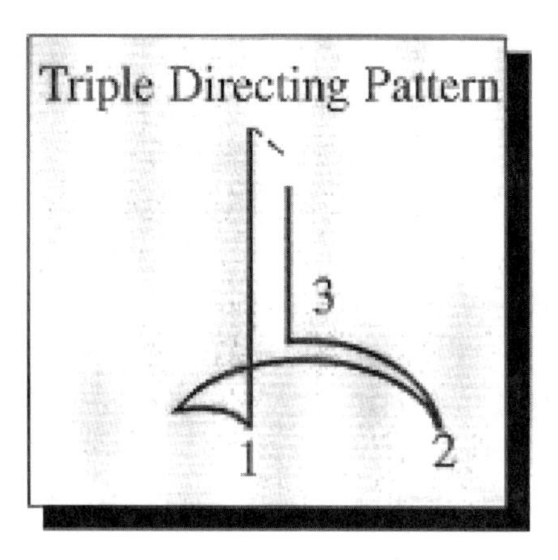

Practice the pattern—down, right, up—until it becomes natural. Tempo and style of articulation depends on the speed and style of the movement. Many of the praise songs and choruses, as well as hymns used in the worship service, can be directed by using the triple pattern.

A third meter to be discussed is quadruple or four-part. This meter is actually a combination of two and two. This meter requires a pattern consisting of four motions—down, left, right, and up (floor, wall, wall, ceiling). The four-part pattern is employed for a majority of the music used in most contemporary worship services. Many of the hymns, gospel songs and choruses fall into quadruple meter or "common time."

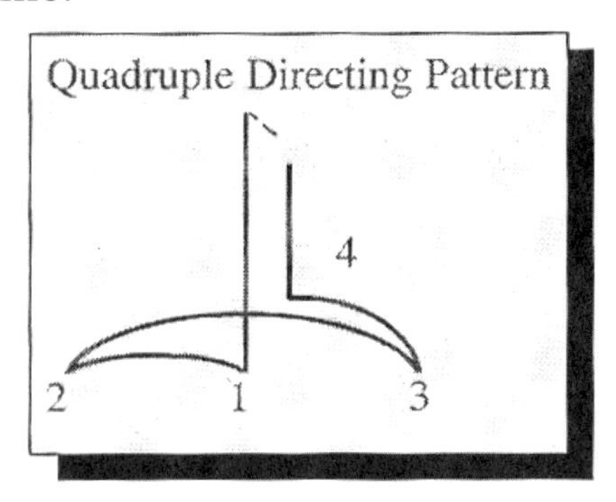

When ending the music performance, the leader's hands stop moving, and the music should end. The leader simply stops the motion, or describes a loop with the hand which stops when the hand comes back to the beginning of the loop. Simplicity and consistency are keys to clarity and consequently, effective worship leading.

The Worship Team

Preparation for leading in worship relates not only to the music minister, but also to each member of the worship or praise team. Their role is to enable worship. When the worship leader is joined by a team of musicians, another dimension of modeling and leading is added to the singing—the understanding of the text and the emotional impact of the music. The role of the worship team becomes one of providing support for the leader. It is not to detract or draw attention to the group. In this role, it is incumbent on the worship team to blend in, not stand out. Visually, they need to be seen as involved together in purpose and presentation. Musically, they need to achieve a blended sound. This musical balance and blend should allow the ensemble to sound like "one voice." There is no place for soloistic performance from any member of the team.

The worship team also needs to be involved creatively, particularly in providing variety in their performance. When singing a happy song, they should look and sound positive and joyful. The music itself will give clues about how to look. If the song is smooth and reflective, the singers should convey that by look and attitude. They should not maintain the same physical stance and look at all times. The singers should not communicate with just one section of the congregation to the exclusion of the whole. They should spread the impact of communication throughout the entire congregation. Leaders should consider wearing a variety of clothes and try not to look the same for every service. Creating variety in message and presentation adds to the probability of achieving meaningful worship.

The Choir as Worship Leader

The use of choirs in leading worship is a long-standing Biblical and historical tradition that seems to be reemerging. In 2 Chronicles 5:11-14, a large choir of priests led worship at the dedication of the Temple, and the glory of the Lord came down and filled the house. A choir that shows extravagant devotion to the Lord and provides direction to the congregation in worship, while singing skillfully in unanimous action and in one accord, will demonstrate effective leadership. Leading anointed worship through music is not just about performance, it is also about passion. It is message and manner of singing. It is also about modeling and spiritual involvement and response.

Choirs have always been important in God's Word and in His work. This concept is demonstrated throughout Scripture in examples like the heavenly choirs singing at the Creation (Job 38); heavenly hosts singing at the birth of Christ (Luke 2); priests singing at the dedication of the Temple (2 Chronicles 5); Jesus and the disciples singing in the Garden (Matthew 26); and by the multitudes who will be worshiping and singing around the throne (Revelation 5). The tradition rightfully continues when believers today join together in choirs around the world and sing songs of praise, worship and salvation. When God does something powerful, He often uses choirs to announce the event. Perhaps, the greatest use of the choir in this generation will be the joyful announcement of salvation for all who would believe and the prophetic proclamation of the imminent return of Christ.

The worship-leading choir is a microcosm of the congregation. As such it becomes a tool for education, evangelism, nurture, and worship a force for spiritual vitality in the church. If there is victory in the choir, it is also in the homes of choir members, thereby permeating the church. If there are problems in the choir, expect problems in the church. If people are being saved, healed, and blessed in the choir, it will spread to the congregation.

The choir leads the congregation in worship and the various acts of praise. Through raised hands, clapping hands, lifted voices, and prayer and praise, one can witness the choreography of the choir enlivening the church. The choir also leads in giving, in sacrifice, in responding to the message, and the call of the Holy Spirit.

The worship-leading choir is continuously involved in demonstrating the reality of the Christian life. Membership in the choir requires personal devotion and dedicated Christian living, portraying the life-changing power available to believers. The music team can show forth Christ by their knowledge, lifestyles and actions.

Choirs are involved in the act of communicating and connecting. It is a responsibility of each choir member to be connected. First, they must connect with God. They must present their bodies a living sacrifice—offering Him their bodies, minds, and spirits. They connect with God by reaching upward. Then they connect with themselves by reaching inward to create and actualize the dream of what they can be and do in the kingdom of God. The choir also connects with others by reaching outward. They reach out to the congregation and communicate the reality of Jesus Christ by leading them in worship and service.

It is time to renew the commitment of the church to the importance of choirs in all its ministries. Churches should spend the time, effort, and resources to establish an effective, anointed choir program that will provide a foundation for effective and anointed music ministry to this "worship generation."

12

The Sacred-Secular Issue

Music is and should be a natural and expected presence in the lifestyle of believers. In listening, performance, and participation, worshipers are able to experience the benefits of various types of music in all aspects of their lives. Without doubt, Christians will be exposed to both sacred and secular music, and it is important to exercise care and caution in evaluating the good and bad aspects of both. Discreet choices are best made after discussion and prayer.

Music and Spiritual Warfare

A discussion of the sacred and secular as it relates to music and spiritual warfare is particularly important in today's cultural and musical environment. Satan, cast out of heaven because of his desire to be equal with God, took with him remarkable skills in many areas perhaps his greatest skill being music. Since that time, he has used music to steal the souls of men and women. He has even become skillful in distorting God's music. Throughout the Christian era, there has developed a tension between music created for performance in church sacred music—and music created for performance outside the church secular music. In determining appropriate usage, the following questions need to be considered: Can only music that is designated as church music be sung in church? What determines whether music is church music? Does music become sacred music when secular music from popular culture finds its way into the church? These questions are not new, and they are important to contemplate.

Early in the Christian church experience, this was not the problem it is today, because the early church tried to create music for worship that was "other worldly" or ethereal in nature. The style of writing and performance was meant to be in contrast to popular or secular music. Singers sang with little vibrato. Musical scales and forms were different from the popular forms of the time. This extreme contrast in sound and style was the practice for several centuries and eventually part of the cause of the laity becoming disinterested and unaccepting of church music.

Martin Luther, reformer, leader and musician, was responsible for instituting significant changes in acceptance of different musical styles for use in the church. He provided for the service to be performed in the vernacular, German as opposed to Latin, and he allowed song texts to be combined with popular melodies of the day. He paired popular and folk melodies with both psalm and hymn texts. These "new songs" were immensely popular with the people and exerted tremendous influence as agents of change during the Protestant reformation. The sacred-secular dichotomy was blurred.

This use of popular melodies in the worship context was both highly successful and controversial. The practice has remained controversial through several centuries, and church musicians and leaders are still grappling with ways to effectively deal with the issue. To be sure, secular music has a tremendous influence on this society often a negative one. Somewhere a teenager is contemplating committing suicide because of the music he or she is listening to. Somewhere a couple is tripping out on the latest drug of choice because of the music they are listening to. Somewhere a family is in danger of breaking up because of the immoral influence of music. Music has a very real influence on feelings, thoughts, and behavior. The following questions need to be considered: What are some ways to deal with this issue effectively? What are the differences between sacred and secular music, and under what circumstances can each be used to provide positive results? How does music communicate with or influence its listeners? Is the appeal of this music primarily intellectual, emotional, spiritual, physical, or even visceral? Will this music help or hurt listeners who are responsible Christians?

Modes of Musical Communication

There are three primary modes or areas of communication through music. Each of these should be given proper consideration.

The first area is intellectual (or head) communication. This is communication in the cognitive domain. In other words, when listening to music, how are the thoughts affected? How does the text influence the listener's rational processes? What kind of visual imagery is created by listening and responding to the music?

The second area of communication is emotional (or heart) communication. This is communication in the affective domain. In other words, what emotions are aroused as one listens to this music? How does one feel listening to this music? What kinds of aesthetic response are present? Is the music beautiful . . . soothing . . . enjoyable . . . worshipful . . . distasteful?

The third area is psychomotor (or visceral) communication. This is communication in the psychomotor domain. Music stimulates the larger muscular responses of the body. What does listening to this music, particularly when it is loud, encourage the listener to do? What kind of physical responses occur?

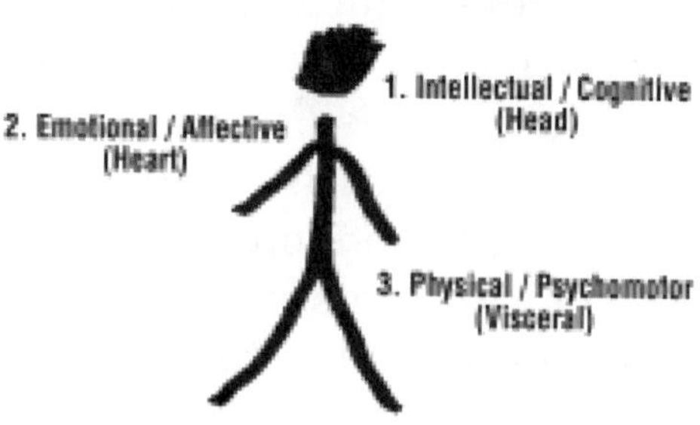

These are important considerations whether talking about music for the church, defined as sacred, or music for life activities, defined as secular. Secular music sometimes makes its way into the church, and sacred music goes outside. Often the lines are blurred in making the right choices concerning the value and appropriateness of both.

Guidelines for Music Choices

The following list of guidelines and questions can be helpful in determining whether a particular music selection, either sacred or secular, is appropriate for Christians and the Christian lifestyle.

First, what is the text (or lyric) of this music saying? One should isolate the words of the text to determine what is actually being communicated. What do the words imply? What are the concepts conveyed? Is this music meant to glorify God? Is it positive and wholesome? Do the words edify and build up, or do they destroy? Does the lyric promote revolution or anarchy? Does it promote a deviant lifestyle? Does this text praise immorality, drugs, or unacceptable behavior? Is there hidden meaning in the text? These questions are central to making informed decisions about music to be used in either a sacred or secular setting.

> A popular song of the '70s, "Lucy in the Sky With Diamonds," stands out in my memory. As I was returning home from church one Sunday, listening to the radio with one of my daughters, I heard that phrase repeated again and again—

> "Lucy in the sky with diamonds." I suddenly realized there was a message coming through that I had not been aware of before. Upon closer examination, I discovered the song was subtly glorifying the beauties of LSD.
>
> Similarly, another incident stands out in my mind. While attending a wedding, I listened as the chorus of a song was repeated with these beautiful words: "I see Jesus in you." As I listened more closely, I began to understand that the verses of the song were saying that people are God, and they commune with Him, not just as humans, but also through the aspects of Godship in them. Here was a New Age theology being presented in a warm and accepting environment.

Whether evaluating sacred or secular music, there is need to understand the text as to meaning and message.

Second, what is the motive (or intended use) of this music? What is the motive of both writer and performer? What is the intended use of this music? Can the listener worship when he hears this music? Does he feel better, or does he feel hostile? Is this music meant to uplift or to tear down? Does this music promote immoral behavior or immoral feelings? Certain music is intended to promote a homosexual lifestyle. Other music glorifies the drug culture, advocates political revolution or promotes destruction of the Judeo-Christian worldview. There are other musical examples that approve deviant sexual practices and lifestyles. Some examples of rap and hip-hop fit this description. Other music is expressly intended to uplift, energize, and promote good thoughts and feelings.

Third, what is the association (or influence) of this music? What associations or mental images stand out as one listens to this music? Does this music take the listener to a far-away place? Is this music reminiscent of former unacceptable activities and behaviors? Does this music bring up thoughts of drugs or evil powers? Does this music provoke thoughts of revolution? Does this music draw one toward God? Does this music provoke positive feelings or thoughts?

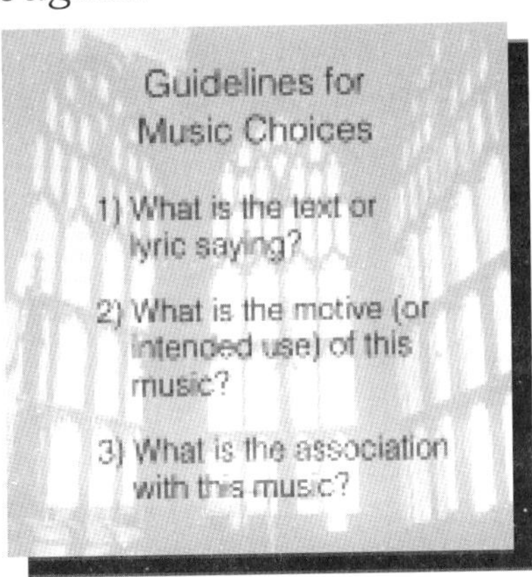

I remember an occasion where I was talking to a group of young people about the evils of certain types of rock music. I told them there were problems with some forms of rock music. I then asked these questions: "Understanding that God created all music, is there such a thing as

Christian rock? Is it all right for Christians to listen to certain kinds of rock, and is it possible for Christian writers to compose rock music?" About halfway through the questions, a young man in the back of the room stood up and said: "I will tell you, sir, that it is not possible for Christians to listen to rock, and there is no such thing as Christian rock music." That stopped me instantly. I did not expect such a response. Needing to respond, I said, "Obviously you have problems with rock music. Tell me why you feel so intensely about this." And he said, "I've been a Christian less than a year. Before I came to know the Lord, I was a rock musician, and I lived a terrible life. I was into everything wrong and undesirable." He recounted behavior that included drug usage, as well as other types of illegal actions. He said, "When I came to the Lord, He changed me, and took me out of the rock culture. I can't ever listen to rock music again, because it makes me want to go back on drugs to a bad lifestyle, and that lifestyle still appeals to me." I looked him in the face and said, "That is precisely the point that I am making. I hope you will never listen to rock music again, because you don't need anything that would tempt you to go back to that lifestyle. For you to listen to Christian rock would be a problem because of the association you have had with that form of music. However, in contrast, my three daughters have never

> been into drugs or other deviant life-styles, and up to this point, they have never even been to a rock concert. They are committed Christians. When they hear Christian rock music, they are listening to the music without any association whatsoever with the things you mentioned. Consequently, they can enjoy music created by Christian rock writers and musicians without associations that will cause them to lose their faith."

If certain types of music cause an individual to want to do something other than that which is good, he should stay away from it. There is no simple yes or no when considering answers to any of these three questions or issues.

Certain music examples might not be appropriate for Sunday morning worship, but they may be very appropriate for the Christian concert or youth fellowship. If the answer is no or negative to all three of the previous questions concerning the acceptability of any specific musical example, then that music can be reasonably considered as inappropriate for Christians. What are the words really saying? What is the intended use of this music? What is the listener's personal association with this music? If one comes to a negative conclusion on all three questions, it can be concluded with assurance that such music does not belong in the life of the believer.

The choice belongs to the individual. Whose drum is he marching to? Whose melody will he listen to? When these criteria are consistently and fairly applied to all music, progress can be made toward using music to influence lives positively in both sacred and secular activities. God wills both for the edification of His people. Satan's disruptive influence must be discovered and prevented in the interest of a return to the well-rounded use of music in worship, evangelism, training, recreation, and nurture.

13

Spiritual Music in the Church

The church has a need for spiritual music—vocal and instrumental—that also has appeal to young and old. The apostle Paul's admonition to be spiritual in all things certainly applies to music in the church. Musical style is not the relevant issue in determining the spiritual nature of music. There have been many crossovers of style and form between the sacred and secular aspects of music. Under some circumstances, this is desirable. Unlike the early Christians, music today is not performed in an ethereal or other worldly manner. Even though much music for today's church is likely to have a popular derivation, there is still need for it to be spiritual in content and motive.

Music That Is Spiritual

It is "not by might, nor by power, but by my spirit, saith the Lord" (Zechariah 4:6). The effectiveness of church music, particularly in the Pentecostal/ Charismatic tradition, is in its spiritual nature. The musician needs to show evidence that he is filled with the Spirit and that he has submitted to the presence, anointing, and guidance of the Holy Spirit. Spirit-filled musicians sing and play as unto the Lord, and their lives resonate with the power and presence of the Spirit.

The purpose of spiritual singing and playing is different. Spiritual singing is not purely aesthetic, or purely for entertainment, or to demonstrate the skills of the musician. Its purpose is not promotion of the worship leader who plays the keyboard skillfully, or who is gifted with a pleasing voice, or knows how to transition from fast to medium to slow, or knows how to conceive impressive modulations and completely control an audience. None of this is the goal of spiritual music. The purpose of spiritual music is to glorify God and enter into His presence to receive blessings. Spiritual singing or playing is not for personal gratification or praise, but to exalt Christ and to edify one another. Musicians use abilities and talents for spiritual purposes. This will draw men and women to Christ and build them up in the faith.

The Power of Spiritual Music

Spiritual music breaks spiritual bondage. In 1 Samuel 16:23, David played before Saul. Depressed and, some say even demented, Saul's spirits were calmed by David's artful music. Because of David's spiritual playing, the bondage of Satan was overcome, and the dissonance in Saul's life was changed to a calm demeanor. Playing and singing under the anointing breaks the yoke of oppression (see Isaiah 10:27). Anointed, spiritual music breaks spiritual bondage; spiritual music brings spiritual victory. There was something unusual and powerful about the sound of the trumpets played on the day the walls of Jericho fell down. They were normal musicians, playing normal instruments, but when at the command of God and anointed by the Spirit, they walked around the wall the seventh time on the seventh day and played their instruments, the walls fell down flat. Victory was achieved through spiritual music. Hosea 2:15 says that God's people would sing new songs of victory as in the days of their youth, as in the day they came up out of Egypt. Anointed singing does indeed bring spiritual victory.

Spiritual music brings the presence of God, because He inhabits the praises of His people. When the musicians and singers perform in an attitude and an atmosphere of praise, they are assured that God comes into their presence. To lift up a song of adoration and honor to Him brings His presence. Believers are instructed to "enter into his gates with thanksgiving, and into his courts with praise" (Psalm 100:4). The Song of Solomon 2:12 predicts a season of singing that will bring believers closer to God. In these end times, believers also are seeing and experiencing spiritual music as it brings them closer to that moment when they will come ultimately into the presence of God.

Spiritual singing uplifts the spirit. Psalm 25:1 declares: "Unto thee, O Lord, do I lift up my soul." David sang when he felt downcast. In Psalm 40, he talks about being in the pits of life, even the miry clay, and discovering that God pulled him up out of his circumstances and established his feet on the rock and put a new song in his mouth, even praise unto God (vv. 2, 3). When God's people need relief from their present circumstances, they can be lifted up in spirit and attitude through spiritual music. Isaiah 61:3 says to exchange "the spirit of heaviness" for the "garment of praise." Believers experience times in their lives when difficulty and sadness seem to crush them. If they believe the Scripture and follow this injunction, they can take off the "spirit of heaviness" and, through the power of spiritual music, "put on a garment of praise."

Spiritual music brings the glory of God. At the dedication of Solomon's Temple, the glory of the Lord came and filled the Temple or place where they were worshiping. When worshipers are singing and playing together, and the Holy Spirit anoints the music, the glory of the Lord will descend and fill the place.

Spiritual music quickens the prophetic word. In 2 Kings 3:11-16, Elisha called for a minstrel to play before he prophesied. This calls to mind the traditional Pentecostal service where the pastor or the preacher usually wants to have powerful, prophetic singing before the sermon. There is Biblical precedence for this practice, and it underscores the importance of music ministry in the church. First Samuel 10:5, 6, indicates that at a Philistine outpost, Saul and a group of prophets would be preceded by lyres, tambourines, flutes, and harps being played before them, and they would be prophesying. Then the Lord told Saul that the Spirit of the Lord would come upon him in power, he would prophesy with the others, and be changed into a different person (v. 6). The anointed music quickened them, and Saul and the prophets prophesied the Word of the Lord. Throughout the Old Testament, musicians went before the army and played and sang before the battle. Often, God used the power of music to defeat the Enemy and give the victory. Martin Luther said, "Satan flees at the power of the Word, but he flees almost as quickly at the power of music."

A New Focus

It may be useful at this point to recall the words of Paul in Philippians 3:12-14 as he admits that he has not learned or achieved it all and declares: "But this one thing I do, forgetting those things which are behind, and reaching forth unto those things that are before, I press toward the mark for the prize of the high calling of God in Christ Jesus." He has determined to get a new start or new focus. Perhaps, this attitude can best be expressed this way: change the focus from past failures or even past successes, and visualize what is going to happen in future ministry. Focus on what can be done for this generation. Focus on God's calling and gifting to do the work of God. Forget about inadequacies, or what has not been achieved, and press toward future successes.

As one changes focus, thought processes begin to change and it becomes easy to think these thoughts: *The music may not be good yet, and the singers are not the most talented. A gifted keyboardist is needed, and the praise team has to be improved. But I serve a great God and I am in partnership with Him. The future is bright, Lord. I believe You will not only give me the desire, but also the abilities, skills, and power to accomplish my calling. I have faith that I will be successful. My calling is secure, and I will not quit. The past is behind me. Now is the time for a new focus. I will press forward and join the race. I will attain the prize of the high calling of Christ.*

Does music of the church need to be different from music of the world today? Yes, emphatically yes, it does. What is the difference? It is not in the melody, but in the message. It is not in the rhythm or harmony, but in the anointing of God. It is the spiritual essence and quality of the music that defines the difference. May all who hear it, come and be changed.

14

The Power of Music

With rapidly expanding technological advances accompanied by a growing sense of spiritual darkness, it is essential to improve the quality and effectiveness of music and worship in the 21st century. In this day of the worldwide Internet, television, film, and both audio and audiovisual recordings in almost every conceivable format, the task of capturing attention is formidable. The church finds itself in competition with the secular world. The issue is not one of fear of competition; it is rather an issue of making the music of the church more relevant, powerful, and effective. We live in a time of power consciousness and dependence on power in all areas of secular life—economics, politics, sports, communications. The church should be busy in demonstrating the power of Christ and of music as it accomplishes its role in the service of God.

The Power of Praise

Music demonstrates the power of praise. Praise to God is not an option; the believer is commanded to praise Him. Psalm 150 says, "Let everything that hath breath praise the Lord. Praise ye the Lord" (v. 6). The psalmist further declares, "His praise shall continually be in my mouth" (34:1). When the believer consistently practices this behavior, the attitude of praise becomes a lifestyle. God manifests Himself in the praise and singing of His people. Praise brings a new perspective. When believers praise Him, joy comes instead of despair, edification rather than condemnation, faith instead of doubt, victory instead of defeat, and peace instead of turmoil. These principles are depicted in Isaiah 61:3 and Zephaniah 3:14-17, where God wills joy and sings with joy over the restoration of His people. If anyone desires an attitude adjustment and a new outlook on life, the power of praise and the praising lifestyle will bring success.

The Power of Proclamation

Music proclaims the power of God. There are many Scriptural examples of musicians and servants of God who, because of their singing or playing, were able to see God do powerful things. Several of these have already been mentioned, i.e., David, Joshua, Paul, and others.

Miracles occur through the power of proclamation. The Spirit lifts up the name of Jesus and brings power to the proclamation of the gospel. In Acts 1:8, the Lord himself says, "But you shall receive power when the Holy Spirit has come upon you; and you shall be witnesses to Me" (*NKJV*).

> In my lifetime, I have witnessed attitudes change and arguments disappear on the wings of music. In one of my private study and devotion times while thinking about the word *witness*, I went to the dictionary to examine its meaning. I was blessed to discover that a witness is someone who has personal cognizance and has seen, touched, heard, or been involved in an action or event. That is what the power of proclamation is about—Christians who stand up and powerfully witness of Jesus Christ from a personal experience. The world needs to see and hear believers who have knowledge of the saving power of Jesus Christ, His healing, and the reality of His promise of a victorious life. It is looking for the demonstration of the power of God in the lives of His people.

The Power of Prophecy

Music conveys the prophetic word. Scriptures state that in the end times, "[God] will pour out [His] spirit upon all flesh" (Joel 2:28). In this time, one can expect vision casting, prophesying of the things to come, and foretelling of the good things God will do for His people. Music is an appropriate medium for expressing the power of the prophetic word today. It is a powerful resource for telling the good news of the gospel. Musicians and ministers are challenged to not only be involved in the priestly ministry, but also in the prophetic ministry as they respond to the challenges and opportunities of this century.

The Challenge

The challenge of the 21st century is to effectively minister the gospel to an increasingly hostile, secular world. The greatest opportunity and challenge is to unveil Christ so that the world can see Him. The world needs to see Him through His Word, and in the life of believers, transforming and sustaining through His power. Music plays a significant role in revealing Christ to the world.

It is time to rend the veil and let the glory of the Lord rise and be revealed. It is time to show Christ to this generation in all of His majesty and as the true Son of God. What a challenge for music ministers to prepare music and musicians to lift Him up so that all men can be drawn to Him.

Music leaders have an opportunity to put on the mantle, accept the calling, and wear the garment of praise as they respond to the challenges of music ministry. They can truly live the lifestyle of praise, and through worship and witness, be bearers of good news.

In Ezekiel 45, the prophet speaks of building a new Temple—the second Temple. He reveals that he saw water coming up from below the threshold of the second Temple. This had not been the case in the first Temple—being located high up on the mountain. Then Ezekiel saw the water coming from below the threshold of the Temple, flowing out from the Temple and down past the gates, past the city, and past Jerusalem in an unending supply that does not stop nor decrease. It flows out of the city and down the hills and into the countryside. He saw the water becoming rivers of living water. Jesus spoke of the same river, flowing from within the temple of the believers' bodies as He tells of "a river of water springing up into everlasting life." Believers' lives do not have to be parched and dry. They can experience an outflow of the rivers of living water. Consider the possible impact of this river of living water—healing, power, grace, nurture and peace—flowing out from within the believer—out into a hurting world in never-ending streams.

Coming Together Through Music

God is calling believers everywhere to come together in a revival of dynamic worship and witness—a coming together that will allow generations to understand and bless one another. It will be a coming together that allows tolerance of differences in styles, traditions, languages, and interests. It will be a coming together that foreshadows the ultimate gathering of believers in the presence of God. It will be a coming together that includes music as a vital ingredient of what God will accomplish through His people.

> During a Sunday morning worship service, I was ministering in a small church with a small choir, singing with soundtrack accompaniment. The keyboardist was also playing along with the tracks. Suddenly, the director, choir and accompanist became intensely involved in the presentation of the message of our music, and the Spirit of the Lord came and powerfully anointed the choir for ministry.
>
> Later, I was in the British Virgin Islands with people of a different culture and tradition. Almost everyone had come to the service either by foot or by boat. The church was crowded and we were in continuous worship for a long time, singing a different style of music, expressing ourselves in a different way physically. The power of the Holy Spirit came and anointed the choir ministry, and people left their seats and came forward to be blessed.
>
> In another service on a Sunday night at a large, urban church, a similar experience occurred. The lighting was different

and the stage was filled with sets, screens, microphones, and monitors. The majority of the audience was under 25—it was a youth-oriented service. There was drama, staging, scenery, movement, and excitement. There were blaring guitars and strange looking costumes. But the message was powerful as the musicians sang from their hearts. The result was a coming of the presence of the Holy Spirit and several commitments to salvation.

Similarly, at a worship conference in the Philippines, I witnessed hours of praise and worship through music, resulting in the presence of God and significant blessings.

Recently, while watching Christian television, I was blessed by the sincere singing of gospel songs from a studio filled with maturing musicians.

I am recalling being in a general convocation in St. Louis with thousands of people, a huge choir, blending with a praise and worship team and orchestra. I heard beautiful sounds of praise ascending up to the Lord, and I saw His glory fill that place. The music and worship sounded like falling rain.

I remember being within 400 yards of the Upper Room with believers from around the world at a Pentecostal World Conference, leading in worship with people of

> all races, traditions, and styles of music. As I sang in English, on one side of me, a believer sung in German, another in Spanish, another in Korean—different languages, but the same melody, and the same expression of praise. It was worship, and the same presence was felt, and the same Holy Spirit came and united the people.

Music born in the heart of God has always been expressed through His creations, and that will never end. Throughout the ages, believers have been united with God in praise and worship. The opportunity to worship in the presence of God will not cease. In Revelation 5:11, 12, the writer portrays heavenly worship as the redeemed gather around the throne of God.

> Then I looked, and I heard the voice of many angels around the throne, the living creatures, and the elders; and the number of them was ten thousand times ten thousand, and thousands of thousands, saying (or singing) with a loud voice: "Worthy is the Lamb who was slain to receive power and riches and wisdom, and strength and honor and glory and blessing" (*NKJV*).

And so God's people will be with the Lord—worshiping, singing, and sharing eternally.

APPENDICES

Glossary

GLOSSARY

A

aesthetic—Beautiful, pleasing in appearance, appreciative of what is pleasing to the senses.

affective—Relating to, arising from, or influencing feelings or emotions; expressing emotion (affective disorders, affective language).

B

bimodal—Having or relating to two modes. (Mode: a particular form or variety of something.)

bridge—A musical passage, linking two sections of a composition.

C

cognitive—Knowing: awareness, understanding, learning, and judgment.

continuum—A coherent whole characterized as a collection, sequence, or progression of values or elements varying by minute degrees.

D

distinctive—Serving to distinguish; characteristics.

duple—Two-part rhythm—two beats or a multiple of two beats per measure.

H

hone—To sharpen; to make more effective.

L

legato—A manner that is smooth and connected; used especially in directing music.

M

microphones

Unidirectional—a microphone used for solo singing, a praise team, or a speaker. The sound goes to the microphone from one direction only.

Omnidirectional—a microphone used for a choir or orchestra. This microphone has a much greater field for receptivity of sound coming from different directions.

minstrel—One of a class of medieval musical entertainers, especially a singer of verses to the accompaniment of a harp; any of a troupe of performers.

P

paradigm—An example or pattern.

prelude—An introductory performance, action, or event preceding and preparing for the principal or more important matter. A musical selection, serving as an introduction.

psychomotor—Of or relating to motor action directly proceeding from mental activity.

Q

quadruple meter—A grouping of four units, organized together, as in four beats or pulsations per measure.

S

shofar—A ram's horn trumpet blown by the ancient Hebrews in battle and high religious observances.

strophic—Using the same music for successive stanzas.

staccato—Cut short or apart in performing; disconnected; marked by short, clear-cut playing or singing of tones or chords.

split-track—A method of recording on both sides (left and right) of a two-track cassette, CD, or DVD where one side has the music for the band and the other side of that two-part track has the singing.

T

tracks—Prerecorded music to assist in learning and performing music in the church.

triple meter—A grouping of three units, organized together, as in three beats or pulsations per measure.

V

visceral—Instinctive; the larger muscular responses of the body.

Bibliographies

BIBLIOGRAPHY OF MUSIC *

"Get Ready." Da'dra Crawford Greathouse, Mark Heimermann, and David Mullen. *Change Our World.* SpiritSound Music Group, Cleveland, Tennessee, © 1999.

"He Must Be in the House." Tim Hill. *Faithful.* Tennessee Music & Printing Co. (a division of SpiritSound Music Group, Cleveland, Tennessee), © 1998.

"Healer in the House." Randy Phillips. *Let the Praises Go Up.* Pathway Music (a division of SpiritSound Music Group, Cleveland, Tennessee), © 1993.

"Healing Grace." Ken Shelton. *Faithful.* Tennessee Music & Printing Co. (a division of SpiritSound Music Group, Cleveland, Tennessee), © 1998.

"He's Been So Good." Devin Stephenson. *Spirit Praise.* His Spirit Music (a division of SpiritSound Music Group, Cleveland, Tennessee), © 1996.

"His Grace Is Sufficient." Myrna Alford. *SpiritSound.* His Spirit Music (a division of SpiritSound Music Group, Cleveland, Tennessee), © 1996.

"Holy Ground." Geron Davis. *Songs for Praise & Worship.* Word Music (a division of Word, Inc.), © 1992.

"Holy Is the Lamb." Randy Phillips. *Spirit Praise.* His Spirit Music (a division of SpiritSound Music Group, Cleveland, Tennessee), © 1996.

"Holy Spirit, Fill Us." Paul Lanier. *The Anointing.* His Spirit Music (a division of SpiritSound Music Group, Cleveland, Tennessee), © 1996.

"I Love You, Lord." Laurie Klein. *Songs for Praise & Worship.* Word Music (a division of Word, Inc.), © 1992.

"I Will Call Upon the Lord." Michael O'Shields. *Songs for Praise & Worship.* Word Music (a division of Word, Inc.), © 1992.

"I Will Praise You." Paul Lanier. *Rejoice.* SpiritSound Music Group, Cleveland, Tennessee, © 2000.

"Joy to the World." Isaac Watts. Public Domain. *The Church Hymnal.* Tennessee Music & Printing Co. (a division of SpiritSound Music Group, Cleveland, Tennessee), © 1951.

"Our God Is Lifted Up." Jeff Switzer. *Rejoice.* SpiritSound Music Group, Cleveland, Tennessee, © 2000.

"Pour Out Your Anointing." Jeff Switzer. *The Anointing.* His Spirit Music (a division of SpiritSound Music Group, Cleveland, Tennessee), © 1996.

"Rejoice and Be Glad." Barry Soots. *Spirit Praise.* His Spirit Music (a division of SpiritSound Music Group, Cleveland, Tennessee), © 1996.

"So Help Me God." Toby McKeeham, Michael Tait, Kevin Smith, Mark Heimermann, and Dann Huff. *Change Our World.* SpiritSound Music Group, Cleveland, Tennessee, © 1999.

"Swing Low, Sweet Chariot." Traditional Spiritual. *The Power of His Presence.* Pathway Music (a division of SpiritSound Music Group, Cleveland, Tennessee), © 1988.

"Tell Them." Rodney K. Elkins. *Rejoice.* SpiritSound Music Group, Cleveland, Tennessee, © 2000.

"The Healer Is Here." David Arivett. *The Anointing.* His Spirit Music (a division of SpiritSound Music Group, Cleveland, Tennessee), © 1996.

"The Potter's Hand." Darlene Zschech. *Change Our World.* SpiritSound Music Group, Cleveland, Tennessee, © 1999.

"We Bow Before You." Paul Lanier. *The Anointing.* His Spirit Music (a division of SpiritSound Music Group, Cleveland, Tennessee), © 1996.

"We Give You Thanks." Jeff Switzer. *The Anointing.* His Spirit Music (a division of SpiritSound Music Group, Cleveland, Tennessee), © 1996.

"We Have a Mission." Geron Davis. *Faithful.* Tennessee Music & Printing Co. (a division of SpiritSound Music Group, Cleveland, Tennessee), © 1998.

"When the Praises Go Up." Randy Phillips. *Let the Praises Go Up.* Pathway Music (a division of SpiritSound Music Group, Cleveland, Tennessee), © 1993.

* All sheet music is used by permission.

BIBLIOGRAPHY OF SOURCES

Alford, Delton, L. *Music in the Pentecostal Church.* Cleveland, Tennessee: Pathway Press, 1967.

Alford, Delton L. "Music in Worship." *Pentecostal Worship.* ed. Cecil B. Knight. Cleveland, Tennessee: Pathway Press, 1974.

Alford, Delton L. "Music, Pentecostal and Charismatic." *The New International Dictionary of Pentecostal and Charismatic Movements* (revised and expanded edition). ed. Stanley B. Burgess. Grand Rapids: Zondervan Publishing, 2002.

Blomgren, David. *The Song of the Lord.* Bible Press, 1978.

Boschman, LaMar. *A Heart of Worship.* Orlando, Florida: Creation House, 1994.

Boschman, LaMar. *The Prophetic Song.* Shippensburg, Pennsylvania: Revival Press, 1986.

Callahan, Kennon L. *Twelve Keys to an Effective Church.* San Francisco: Harper, 1987.

Ellsworth, D.P. *Christian Music in Contemporary Witness*. Grand Rapids: Baker Book House, 1979.

Etherington, C.L. *Protestant Worship Music*. New York: Holt, Rinehart, and Winston, 1962.

Hayford, Jack, John Killinger, and Howard Stevenson. *Mastering Worship*. Portland, Oregon: Multnomah, 1990.

Hooper, L. *Church Music in Transition*. Nashville: Broadman Press, 1963

Hunter, George C. III. *How To Reach Secular Young People*. Nashville: Abingdon Press, 1992.

Lovelace, Austin and William C. Rice. *Music and Worship in the Church*. rev. ed. Nashville: Abingdon, 1976.

Osbeck, K.W. *The Ministry of Music*. Grand Rapids: Zondervan Publishing House, 1961.

Owens, Bill. *The Magnetic Music Ministry*. ed. Herb Miller. Nashville: Abingdon Press, 1996.

Reynolds, William Jensen. *A Survey of Christian Hymnody*. New York: Holt, Rinehart and Winston, Inc., 1963.

Sorge, Bob. *Exploring Worship.* Canandaiqua, New York: Bob Sorge, 1987.

Stevenson, Robert M. *Patterns of Protestant Church Music.* Durham, North Carolina: Duke University Press, 1953.

Stevenson, Robert M. *Protestant Church Music in America.* New York: W.W. Norton & Company, Inc., 1966.

Thomas, Edith Lovell. *Music in Christian Education.* Nashville: Abingdon Press, 1953.

Walker, Paul L. *The Ministry of Worship.* Cleveland, Tennessee: Pathway Press, 1981.

Webber, Robert E. *Planning Blended Worship.* Nashville: Abingdon Press, 1998.

Webber, Robert E. *Worship Is a Verb.* Waco, Texas: Word Books, 1985.

Whittesey, Federal Lee. *A Comprehensive Program of Church Music.* Philadelphia: Westminster Press, 1957.

Index

Index

A

B

C

D

E

F

G

H

I

J

K

L

M

N

O

P

Q

R

S

T

U

V

W